In a day when a clear understanding of authority is urgently needed, John Kitchen has provided God's people with a concise and comprehensive book on the subject. The warm style is spiritually and intellectually stimulating. The reader will catch the passion of a pastor for his family, flock and the church-at-large to have a balanced view of authority. The exceptional sections on delegated authority make the book a must for the pastor's library. The essence of leadership is captured in the volume and should be considered by all aspiring to the role.

Gary Benedict
President, Crown College,
St. Bonifacius, Minnesota

As a resident of a planet thoroughly saturated with self-centeredness run amok, I can think of few topics needing to be discussed more than that of authority. Thankfully, John Kitchen offers a wonderful blend of insights into the current values and behaviors that reject the premise of authority, and then gives a strong biblical response. While both immensely readable and practical, this book offers an excellent model of how one must analyze and synthesize biblical theology and apply it to life. This is a solid apologetic for the concept of authority that should be read and passed along by ministers and Christian leaders everywhere.

Donald L. Hamilton
Stephen F. Olford Professor of Preaching
Columbia Biblical Seminary

The critical issue in the ministry of Jesus was: 'By what authority are you doing these things?' (Luke 20:2). I heartily commend Dr. John Kitchen's thoughtful and unique treatise. He has given us a very practical book in which he makes the case for the commanding authority of God and his Word in times like ours. He explores the derived authorities such as government, church, home (marriage and parents). I do not know of any book just like this treatment and would commend it as a discussion volume for an adult class or small group discussion. This book is eminently Scriptural, relentlessly practical and very well-written. I wholeheartedly recommend it.

David L. Larsen,
Trinity Evangelical Divinity School

John A. Kitchen's *Embracing Authority* is a thoroughly counter-cultural, transformingly revolutionary, and deeply Christian re-appraisal of the good and wise gift of God-ordained authority structures. The egalitarian impulse of our age follows our sinful urges in rebelling against the relationships of authority within which our lives find fullest and freest expression. Kitchen calls us back to submit to God's mandate of submission and authority in all, but in only, the ways God has designed for his glory and for our highest well-being and joy.

Bruce A. Ware, President
Council on Biblical Manhood and Womanhood

Embracing Authority

Learning to Live Joyfully in God's World

John A. Kitchen

Christian Focus

© John A Kitchen
ISBN 1 857 92 715 X

Published in 2002
by
Christian Focus Publications,
Geanies House, Fearn, Ross-shire,
IV20 1TW, Great Britain

Cover design by Alister MacInnes

Printed and bound in Great Britain by
The Guernsey Press Co. Ltd., Guernsey, Channel Islands

Contents

Preface 7

1 An Aversion to Authority 9

2 The Authority of God 25

3 The Authority of God and his Word 41

4 The Authority of God and the Government..... 61

5 The Authority of God and the Church 77

6 The Authority of God and Marriage 97

7 The Authority of God and Parenthood 117

8 The Authority of God and the Believer 135

9 The Authority of God and Preaching............. 153

10 The Authority of God and the Great
    Commission.. 175

11 The Authority of God and Servanthood 191

12 The Authority of God and the Close of
    History 203

Subject Index... 213

This volume is dedicated with
deep appreciation to

ALLEN SPARKS

... who is my pastor, and mentor and friend.
... who exercises authority without becoming enamoured with it.
... who models the spiritual authority of a servant's heart.

Preface

One of the greatest cinema innovations of our time will prove to have been the film *Jurassic Park*, another of Steven Spielberg's masterfully produced projects. The story line is intriguing – the technology of the present has not only been able to bring to life the dinosaurs of old, but also has been able to keep them safely under wraps in a specially designed facility. It is a tale of the prowess of progress over the perils of the past. A great story, that is, until something goes terribly wrong and the monsters of the past run amuck and the pioneers of progress must scramble to regain control.

Children seem to love the film for its dinosaurs. I see, however, a deeper message in the film. At the risk of being overly analytical, I believe that we are trapped in something of a moral Jurassic Park. No, Tyrannosaurus Rex is not roaming the countryside threatening to devour homes, frightening small children and generally disrupting the peace. We are, however, with all of our technological advancement, unable to shake the monsters of the past – monsters like greed, violence, selfishness, immorality, idolatry, addictions, and the occult, to name just a few. For all of our progress we have never truly been able to tame these monsters of our past. The fact is they have never really been behind us at all. Rather, they have walked side by side with us as we have 'progressed' to the advanced state in which we find ourselves today.

At root are the twin issues of authority and power. We would love to believe we have, or, given enough time will soon discover the power to deal with our own problems. Just a few more dollars for research, just another year or two of post-graduate work, just a little more tax money for bigger programs and we will have these monsters licked. We fail to see, however, that we will never have the power necessary to overcome our problems because we lack the authority to do so. Lack of power is not our problem. Lack of power within ourselves, yes. But lack of available power to deal with our problems? No. Power aplenty exists to conquer the monsters of our past. We simply do not possess the authority to exercise that power.

We fancy ourselves to be autonomous, free creatures. Authority is out! Yet, if we will believe the biblical analysis of things, we are now, and always have been, under authority. Our grand proclamations of autonomy are but the boastful squeaks of tiny creatures in the hand of an infinite God. That horizon just ahead, that we believe we can conquer and over whose crest, we are convinced, lie the answers to our problems, is but another fold in the unbounded palm of the the Master.

If we are ever to conquer the monsters that have plagued us from our beginnings, we must willingly come again under the authority of God. Few propositions sound as revolting to man, but only when we come under his authority will he release his power and the authority we need to wield it against the monsters that have ruled us. The pages that follow are a humble attempt to assert the reality of the sovereign authority of God. Without a fresh appreciation of it we will be consumed.

We will begin our quest by examining the nearly irreversible vortex of rebellion against God's authority. Then against the backdrop of a fresh look at God's sovereign authority, we will attempt to set forth the ways in which God has delegated his authority for the administration of the universe he created. I include an analysis of how delegated authorities should function under God's absolute authority. We will conclude by examining how authority is related to the very purposes of the universe and points us to God's climactic conclusion for human history.

May God be praised as the unrivalled Ruler of the Universe that he is. May this feeble attempt in some way promote his praise.

1

An Aversion to Authority

There is only one throne ... and God is on it. Period. A pluralistic, relativistic world squirms under such dogmatic assertions. The bumper sticker has been around for decades, but it continues to speak the heart-cry of many even today: 'Question Authority!' Woe to the man, woman or child who questions the authority to make such a bold declaration! An entire culture stands ready to defend its assertion.

Authority, and particularly submission to it, is not in vogue. The fact is it never has been. Our culture is racing head-long in its militant defiance of any authority. The apostle Paul warned us about the break-neck speed with which rebellion would advance in the last days. 'But realize this, that in the last days difficult times will come. For men will be lovers of self, lovers of money, boastful, arrogant, revilers, disobedient to parents, ungrateful, unholy, unloving, irreconcilable, malicious gossips, without self-control, brutal, haters of good, treacherous, reckless, conceited, lovers of pleasure rather than lovers of God' (2 Tim. 3:1-4, NASB).

Rebellion has come to be venerated as one of the undeniable rights of a free society. Rebels are ushered to the throne, where they are deified and conferred with the authority to enforce non-conformity. Rebellion is 'in'.

We need little help to see the popularity of the rejection of authority and the penchant for rebellion. Consider, however, a recent article in a Chicago-based magazine. The article was entitled 'Buy Hip' and chronicled how the advertizing world can now sell anything if it can be cast in a motif of rebellion.

Mentioned in the article is Spike Lee, the film innovator who has become something of a cult hero, known for his free-floating radical views. Mr. Lee lobbies the rulers of the popular culture as a spokesman for the country's oppressed. Spike is an outspoken opponent of morality as America has traditionally known it. The shoe manufacturing powerhouse, NIKE, has seized upon Mr. Lee's image and paraded him across the television screen in their shoes. Such will sell.

Burger King adopted an advertizing scheme that boasts: 'Sometimes you gotta break the rules.' There is the perfume called Tribe that woos its consumers with a call to 'Join the uprising'. Mazda tells us, 'You're not John Doe, why drive his car?' Tennis star Andre Agassi sells a camera called 'The Rebel' under the slogan 'Image is everything'. James Dean, famed for his portrayal of a young deviant in the film *Rebel Without a Cause*, has made a comeback from the grave. His 'I don't care' image is emblazoned everywhere. I can recall driving through downtown Milwaukee and passing the Koss headphone factory. The billboard along the freeway peddled their wares with a picture of Dean sporting a pair of their headphones and then under the picture the slogan 'Rebel With a Koss'.

T. C. Frank, author of the article, says, 'The commercialization of deviance is fast becoming the universal motif of our age.... So American youth and its young-thinking parents fall over one another rushing to patronize the latest consumer expression of rebellion, whether it's acid-washed jeans, leather motorcycle jackets, or multiple-pierced ears. We let our hair grow, cut it short, tie it in a ponytail, dye it, cut lines and words into it. We wear all black. We purchase every new product, visit every new nightclub we think will set us apart from the crowd, and exemplify our daring disdain for tradition. And then a few months later we do it all over again, with other products and other places.'[1]

Rebellion is big business. The reason it sells is that it is a part of our nature. 'Wait a minute!' someone protests. 'Not so fast! You say this is part of human nature. That rebellion is something bad, something bad that we are going to be held responsible for. That is not true! First, I am not so sure rebellion is bad at all. Second, I believe I can prove to you that rebellion is not inborn.'

Who would buy such a line? A good many Americans would. Consider the argumentation put forward in a recent book by Frank J. Sulloway. Mr. Sulloway's book, *Born to Rebel: Birth Order, Family Dynamics, and Creative Lives*, proposes to find a different root from which rebellion is said to spring.[2] For Mr. Sulloway, rebellion is not an inborn part of fallen human nature pushing and shoving to keep its distance from God. Rather, rebellion is due to one's birth order. Far from being sin for which one will be held accountable before the Judge of the universe, rebellion is the creative genius molded into the lives of leading people who are willing to colour outside the lines. The molding takes place in their environment, particularly their order of birth and place in the family structure in which they grew up. Firstborns are more moralistic and given to activism, those born in the middle of the pack are more prone to make concessions on important points, while the children born later are visionaries. So, you see, a person is not to be held responsible for rebellion. It is not their fault. They are but a product of their environment. Neither should we consider rebellion a negative thing. Not at all – many of the greatest advances have been made by people who were labeled as rebels by their generation. To support his claims Sulloway surveyed scientific, religious, political and social history to identify later-born rebels who helped shape our world.

Creative as his theory is, Mr. Sulloway stands in an already-too-long line of people frantically attempting to shift personal responsibility on to someone else. Be it arguments for genetic based 'causes' for everything from alcoholism to homosexuality or Mr. Sulloway's attempt to redefine and redirect the nature of rebellion, all attempts at escape from our culpability before our Creator are lame at best. Fortunately some of Sulloway's reviewers have uncovered the inherent

11

self-protective bias in his writings. Even so the blame-shifting bred in the Garden (Gen. 3:12-13) lives on today.[3]

We who reside behind the cover of stained glass must beware of presuming the problem is one that exists simply 'out there'. The prophetic call of A. W. Tozer in his searching editorial 'The Waning Authority of Christ in the churches' is as searing today as when it first appeared. Ours is not normally the brazen defiance of the culture at large. Yet the mutant form that lays aside the leather and chains and dons the sport coat and Bible-cover springs from the same root. For all of its polished sanctification it is still at its core a putrid and foul odor in the nostrils of a sovereign, holy King.

Tozer should be heard again: 'Let me state the cause of my burden. It is this: Jesus Christ has today almost no authority at all among the groups that call themselves by his name.... All authority is his in heaven and in earth. In his own proper time he will exert it to the full, but during this period in history he allows this authority to be challenged or ignored. And just now it is being challenged by the world and ignored by the church.'[4]

What is active rebellion in the world is passive disinterest in the church. The pious look down their noses and run from the one while they embrace the other amidst the waning strains of a praise chorus and, if one looks closely enough, you just might spot a tear falling from the corner of their eye. Both forms of rebellion reek of pride, arrogance, and the spirit of malcontent. Both grieve the heart of God. God is not fooled by our intricately woven covering of sanctity.

Once again we are forced to admit that, inside and outside of the church, human nature, that is, what comes naturally, is now being ushered to the throne and given the scepter that it might rule the day.

May we, however, stop the coronation march just long enough to raise a question? Is rebellion good for us? Yes, it comes from within. It is natural. But is it good for us? Is authority wrong? Don't answer too quickly. Is authority wrong

... always? To be sure, we have ample illustrations of those who grasp after and abuse authority. There have always been the likes of Jim Jones, David Koresh, Idi Amin, and Nicolae Ceausescu. People fear 'big government'. Politicians are drawn by the social commentators of the day as buffoons intent only on their own self-preservation and pleasure. The line of abusers-of-authority is a long one, running so far back in time that it disappears on the horizon of history past.

May I still venture to ask: Is that reason enough to cast aside authority? The mirror of God's Word betrays the fact that we have become a teeth-gritting, clench-fisted, nose-in-the-air, defiant society. I want to suggest that the price we are paying for it is far too high.

There is one throne, and God is on it! When we try to play King of the hill with the King of kings we will not escape without destructive consequences. The rubble of the war is all around us: violent crime, domestic abuse, divorce, drug abuse, unwanted pregnancies, abortion, and on and on the list could go.

It will be our intent in this book to consider the biblical expression of the authority that belongs to God alone. However, before we begin that venture we need to stop and examine the flip side of that authority. What is this thing we call rebellion? What does it look like? How can I spot it ... in myself and in others?

To answer those questions we can do no better than to consider Israel's first king – Saul. Saul was the darling of the people; a prince that came to power through the petitions of the people. Saul stood, literally, head and shoulders above his peers. Humanly speaking he had every resource for success. However, soon after the coronation parade was finished, Saul showed his true colours.

Samuel, God's spokesman and the reluctant servant God used to anoint the people's choice for king, came to Saul and announced: 'I am the one the LORD sent to anoint you king over his people Israel; so listen now to the message of the

LORD' (1 Sam. 15:1). The word of the Lord is always the watershed that differentiates rebellion from righteousness. The entrance of the knowledge of God's will leaves us with two clear opportunities – rebellion or obedience. How we work to demand additional options! In the final analysis they simply do not exist.

'This is what the LORD Almighty says: "I will punish the Amalekites for what they did to Israel when they waylaid them as they came up from Egypt. Now go, attack the Amalekites and totally destroy everything that belongs to them. Do not spare them; put to death men and women, children and infants, cattle and sheep, camels and donkeys"' (vv. 2-3). Here is where 'culturally sensitive' people raise an eyebrow. How could God demand such a thing? How could a 'reasonable' God ask one of his own to do something so cruel? The fact is that more people today probably struggle over God's apparent 'arrogance' and inability to deal patiently with those who 'disagree' than they do Saul's impending rebellion against the word of the sovereign Lord of the universe. 'How unlike God!' someone will assert about God's own command. As Dale Ralph Davis puts it, 'Some readers, however, are bothered not with Saul's partial obedience but with Yahweh's severe command.'[5] If we have ears to hear we will realize how this sentiment betrays our comfort with the reasoning of rebellion.

For those delicate types among us, whose sensibilities are offended by the seeming harshness of God's command, realize that God is perfectly justified in his actions toward the Amalekites. It is a matter of record that Amalek initiated the divide with Israel. In fact they launched their attack before Israel ever made it to Sinai (Exod. 17:8-16). Poised to enter the promised land, Moses remembered the viciousness of their attack, 'When you were weary and worn out, they met you on your journey and cut off all who were lagging behind; they had no fear of God' (Deut. 25:18). Indeed God's command here in 1 Samuel 15 to deal thoroughly with Amalek was no whim of the Divine, but had been a longstanding requirement of the people of God (Deut. 25:19). In addition, the spiritual and moral condition of the Amalekites had not changed during the intervening three hundred years (1 Sam. 15:18, 33).[6]

All appeared well as Saul mustered the troops and prepared to attack (vv.4-5). He even graciously gave an opportunity for the innocent to be removed before the wrath of God fell (v.6). The apparent success heightens as we read, 'Then Saul attacked the Amalekites all the way from Havilah to Shur, to the east of Egypt' (v.7). The good news ends here. What remains is the sad record of royal rebellion.

The scent of disobedience is only slightly covered by the perfume of spirituality as we read, 'he took Agag king of the Amalekites alive, and all his people he totally destroyed with the sword. But Saul and the army spared Agag and the best of the sheep and cattle, the fat calves and lambs – everything that was good. These they were unwilling to destroy completely, but everything that was despised and weak they totally destroyed' (vv.8-9).

The first hint of rebellion is seldom heard by those who reject God's authority. Rather it begins with a deep grief in the heart of God himself and is then announced to those who honour his word. 'Then the word of the LORD came to Samuel: "I am grieved that I have made Saul king, because he has turned away from me and has not carried out my instructions." Samuel was troubled, and he cried out to the LORD all that night' (vv.10-11). We will return shortly to this deep wound in God's heart, but for the moment do not allow yourself to pass lightly over the grievous thing rebellion is.

Rebellion demands confrontation, painful as it is, so Samuel, after a sleepless night of agonized prayer, sought out the self-satisfied Saul (v.12). As the prophet sought the king, he received word that Saul, in the wake of his 'victory', had busied himself with establishing his greatness ('he has set up a monument in his own honor') and frosted it with a trip to a worship service (he 'has turned and gone on down to Gilgal', the place where he had been anointed king, 11:14-15).

As the reign of Saul unravels throughout the remainder of the account, notice if you will the traits of rebellion evidenced in Saul. Rebellion has no aversion to religion. Rebellion is at home in robes of righteousness. Normally we picture black leather, chains, body piercing, tattoos, and the like when the word rebellion is spoken. Certainly those things may be one expression of rebellion. Yet the more hideous expressions of rebellion do nothing to look outwardly defiant. Rebellion, particularly the kind most of us reading this book need to concern ourselves with, often dresses itself in choir robes, business suits and pretty dresses. Rebellion can carry a Bible to church and don a pious look upon its face as easily as spirituality can.

'When Samuel reached him, Saul said, "The LORD bless you! I have carried out the LORD's instructions." But Samuel said, "What then is this bleating of sheep in my ears? What is this lowing of cattle that I hear?" Saul answered, "The soldiers brought them from the Amalekites; they spared the best of the sheep and cattle to sacrifice to the LORD your God, but we totally destroyed the rest"' (vv.13-15). The most subtle and insidious rebellion is quick to cast itself in the most spiritual of lights. Again in verse 21 Saul claims, 'The soldiers took sheep and cattle from the plunder, the best of what was devoted to God, in order to sacrifice them to the LORD your God at Gilgal.'

Do not be fooled. Rebellion is most vile when dressed for 'worship'. Rebellion can be found in the small talk in the church foyer ('Did you hear about ...?', 'Oh we do need to be praying for pastor, did you hear that he ...?', 'It is such a shame the church has not responded to ...!') as commonly as in the clatter of the bar down the street. It should be no surprise to us. 'Satan himself masquerades as an angel of light. It is not surprising then, if his servants masquerade as servants of righteousness' (2 Cor. 11:14-15). Indeed even the incarnation of rebellion will himself be one of the most 'religious' people ever known (2 Thess. 2:3-4, 8-10).

Rebellion, for all of its religious trappings, in its heart loathes obedience. Obedience is an emetic to a rebel heart. A rebel simply cannot stomach honest obedience to authority. A clear word from God draws an automatic, sometimes violent reaction.

The biblical narrator tipped off the true heart condition of Saul when he said he and his men 'were not willing' to fully carry out God's command (v.9). Here is rebellion disrobed, with its iron defiance exposed to the world. Saul did not want to obey. Behind the sanctified smile he was not willing to go God's way. He had no intention of carrying out God's instructions. The root and source of all sin is the iron will set against God. The Bible calls it lawlessness (1 John 3:4).

Oh, how our world reacts against that glaring light of truth! The culture of victimhood has little place for the kind of personal responsibility required by a biblical definition of sin. Popular psychology has emasculated the will. 'I can't' is the cry of most when called to control their behavior. We have willfully forgotten that where God issues a command there is the Divine assumption that there is ability to fulfill that command. In a world filled with sin, violence, hatred and self-preservation there are many victims. Unfortunately we have allowed the reality of victimization to con us into the facade of the chained will. 'I can't' is in reality, more often than not, 'I won't'.

But rebellion will not go down so easily. 'I have carried out the LORD's instructions,' Saul cried (v.13). When questioned as to why he did not obey God's instructions, Saul demanded, 'But I did obey the LORD ... I went on the mission the LORD assigned me. I completely destroyed the Amalekites ...' (v.20). I have had to challenge far too many people with sweet, smiling Christian faces who have been caught just as red-handed as Saul had been caught. The word 'sin' is easy to spell in theology class, it is hard to articulate in personal confession. Woe to the one who does not read the 'off limits'

17

sign that accompanies that sweet smile and chooses rather to press a bit further with probing questions. The docile demeanor can quickly transform into violent self-defense if need be. 'I can't get along with my wife!' 'I can't communicate with my husband!' 'I can't discipline my children!' 'I can't give up the affair!' 'I can't stop overeating!' 'I can't find time to pray!' 'I can't ...'

The story is told of an elderly Scottish woman who traveled the countryside peddling housewares for a living. Being a woman of faith, whenever she came to a fork in the road she would take a stick, toss it in the air and whichever way it pointed when it landed was the direction she would proceed in. The woman became rather renowned among the local residents for her bizarre behavior. One day, however, someone saw her at a fork in the road. She took her stick and threw it into the air and watched it land. She then gathered up the stick and proceeded to toss it in the air once again. Looking puzzled at the stick, she picked it up and threw it up one more time. This happened several more times before finally the woman picked up the stick and headed down one of the paths. The bystander's curiosity got the better of him and he asked the woman, 'Why did you do that more than once?' The woman said simply, 'Oh, it kept pointing to the road on the left and I wanted to go the other way because it looks so much smoother.'

Will has its methods to get its way and yet maintain its image of spirituality. Rebellion is capable of balancing both religious impression and the loathing of obedience.

Finally, however, Saul was presented with undeniable evidence that he had indeed not fully obeyed God. The sound of bleating sheep and the nudge of cattle wandering about their legs was hard to ignore (v.14). Unfortunately, blame bounces well off of undeniable evidence. '*The soldiers* brought them ... *I* did obey the LORD ... *I* completely destroyed the Amalekites ... *The soldiers* took sheep and cattle from the plunder ...' (vv.15, 21, emphasis mine).

Blame-shifting is the national sport for the rebellious. It has been happening since the voice of God asked two huddled figures hiding behind a shrub, 'Who told you that you were naked? Have you eaten from the tree that I commanded you not to eat from?' (Gen. 3:11). *'The woman you put here* with me – *she* gave me from the tree, and I ate it.... *The serpent* deceived me, and I ate' (Gen. 3:12-13, emphasis mine).

It is her fault. It is God's fault. It is his fault. 'It has to be someone's fault!' Such is the cry of desperation in the face of undeniable evidence. Rebellion squirms and wiggles under conviction. It is slippery. Defiance always has its bony finger in someone's face.

The following anonymous poem well describes the tragic nature of 'Passing the Buck'.

College Professor:
　'Such rawness in a student is a shame;
　poor high school preparation is to blame.'

High School Principal:
　'Its plain to see the boy's a perfect fool!
　The fault lies strictly with the grammar school.'

Grammar School Teacher:
　'I would that from such dolts I might be spared;
　they send them up to me so unprepared!'

Kindergarten Teacher:
　'Ne'er such a lack of training did I see!
　What sort of person can that mother be?'

Mother:
　'You stupid child! But then, you're not to blame;
　your father's folks I know are all the same!'

Rebellion hides behind phrases like 'Well I'm not perfect!' Or 'I'm as big a sinner as the next guy!' Whatever the particular phrase, it is always followed by 'but!'. Vague,

19

general words of contrition, teary moments of apparent remorse, even confessions carefully crafted so as to never actually admit culpability are the chameleon-like camouflage of rebellion under pressure.

Rebellion has a remarkable ability to see what it wants to see and to hear what it wants to hear. Careful selection of the facts is a skill essential to all who will excel in rebellion. Walter Wink has demonstrated scientifically our ability to see what we want to see with our physical organs of sight. He developed a stereoscope in which he placed two different images. Before the left eye was a picture of a bullfighter while before the right eye was the image of a baseball player. The test group for his experiment was made up of a combination of citizens of Mexico and others from America. Both images were projected before the eyes of each individual. When the Mexican subjects were asked to identify what they saw when looking through the stereoscope the majority of them said, 'I see a bullfighter.' The same question was put to the American participants and the majority of them said, 'I see a baseball player.' The same two images simultaneously picked up by the retina, but only one registered consciously on the brain.[7] We see what we want to see!

Saul certainly was selective with his facts when it came to evaluating his obedience to God. When, in the face of countless sheep and cattle all about them, Samuel pointed out his failure to utterly destroy everything as God had said, Samuel was incredulous. The king didn't see sheep. He saw sacrifices! When Saul insisted 'I did obey the LORD' (v.20) he was impervious to the fact that he had only partially obeyed God's command.

That, however, is the nature of rebellion – it sees what it wants to see and hears what it wants to hear. It was no different in Jesus' day. When the crowds looked upon him they all saw the same Person, but the spiritually hungry perceived a Savior in their midst while the spiritually haughty declared a sinner had arrived.

When asked if being blind was not the worst thing in the world, Helen Keller smiled and said, 'To be blind is bad, but worse is it to have eyes and not to see.'[8] Rebellion lives and moves and has its being in the sad world of illusion. Rebellion hears the same words, its ears catch the same air waves, the same images land on its retina as upon everyone else's, but rebellion hears what it wants to hear and sees what it wants to see.

The Holy Spirit, through the prophet Samuel, kept probing until Saul was at last backed into a corner and confessed. 'I have sinned. I violated the LORD's command and your instructions. I was afraid of the people and so I gave in to them' (v.24).

'Praise the Lord! The breakthrough we have prayed for has come!', the undiscerning may be tempted to conclude. But had repentance truly come? Saul begged to be allowed to worship the Lord (v.25). All appears well. If only Saul had held his tongue, we would never have known better. 'I have sinned. But please honor me before the elders of my people and before Israel' (v.30).

Rebellion is more concerned with appearances than holiness. If only the facade can remain in place. If only others don't have to know. If only the show can go on. Rebellion, at all costs, must maintain the image. 'Image is everything' is not an advertizing slogan invented at the close of the second millennium, it has been around since at least the middle of the second millennium B.C. The apostle Paul spoke of those 'having a form of godliness but denying its power' (2 Tim. 3:5). Again he warned young Titus, 'They claim to know God, but by their actions they deny him' (Tit. 1:16).

Finally rebellion is absorbed with self. There it is, the bottom line. Rebellion will play king of the hill with anyone or anything, even God himself, if he stands in the way of self-interest. Was that not the essence of rebellion's entrance into the universe? 'You said in your heart, "*I will* ascend to heaven; *I will* raise my throne above the stars of God; *I will* sit

21

enthroned on the mount of assembly, on the utmost heights of the sacred mountain. *I will* ascend above the tops of the clouds; *I will* make myself like the Most High"' (Isa. 14:13-14, emphasis mine). Was that not what was at issue when sin entered the human race? 'you will be like God' (Gen. 3:5). Has that not been our fundamental problem ever since? To the place where now month by month we race to the newsstands to gather up a slick, multi-colored publication called simply 'Self!'

It was no different for Saul. Indeed, when Samuel inquired as to Saul's whereabouts, he discovered he had gone to Carmel to erect a monument in his own honor (1 Sam. 15:12). The poetic conclusion to the matter was stated by the prophet: Saul's problem was insubordination and arrogance (v.23). David Larsen has written, 'At the center of "sin" is that proud perpendicular pronoun "I"! There it is, unbent and unbowed, the assertion of self in rebellion and revolt against a holy God.'[9]

That certainly was the essence of Saul's problem and it most certainly is the heart of our current demise.

'Rebellion is like the sin of divination [witchcraft, AV], and arrogance like the evil of idolatry,' said Samuel (v.23). What does that mean? It means that there is but one throne and God is on it. If you choose not to submit to his authority you have chosen to attempt to live in God's world without God. In that dangerous proposition you have opened yourself to the influence of the evil one.

You may never don the black robes of Satanism, but, if you are not bowed absolutely under God's authority, your heart has been blackened by the soot of rebellion against the only legitimate authority in the universe. Harden your heart and you will come under the influence of Satan and his henchmen. Give Satan an inch, and he will attempt to take a mile. He will exploit that tiny, innocently given place and make it a base of operations to gain further ground in that life.

There is a 'No Vacancy' sign hanging on the throne of the universe. We must come under that authority, both in its undiluted form and where it has been delegated. If we do not, we have, by trying to mount the throne of our own life, actually abdicated it in some measure to Satan. Living in God's world without God is to live in misery.

NOTES

1. T. C. Frank, 'Buy Hip', (Chicago: *The Baffler*, 1992) excerpted in *Utne Reader*, July/August, 1992, pp.102, 103.

2. Frank J. Sulloway, *Born to Rebel: Birth Order, Family Dynamics, and Creative Lives* (Pantheon, 1996).

3. See for example Alan Wolfe, 'Up From Scientism', *The New Republic*, December 23, 1996, pp.29-35.

4. A. W. Tozer, 'The Waning Authority of Christ in the churches', in *The Best of A. W. Tozer*, compiled by Warren W Weirsbe (Harrisburg, Pennsylvania: Christian Publications, Inc., 1978), p.88.

5. Dale Ralph Davis, *1 Samuel, Looking on the Heart*, (Christian Focus Publications, 2000), p.124.

6. Ibid., p.13.

7. J. Robertson McQuilkin, *Understanding and Applying the Bible* (Chicago: Moody Press, 1983), p.191.

8. Edythe Draper, *Draper's Book of Quotations for the Christian World* (Wheaton, Illinois: Tyndale House Publishers, Inc., 1992), p.341.

9. David L. Larsen, 'The Transformation of a Terrorist,' in *The Voice From the Cross*, Richard Allen Bodey, ed., (Grand Rapids: Baker Book House, 1990), p.30.

2

The Authority of God

It was a frightening day for a young father. It was the day a certain young girl, who shall remain anonymous except to say that she lives within the same home as me and bears my last name, made a new and rather startling declaration to her father. She straightened her little spine and said, 'I don't have to do what you say!'

That beautiful little blonde-haired, blue-eyed girl could not even say the word 'autonomy' and to my knowledge the concept had never consciously entered her mind before. Yet here I was, realizing for the first time my need to teach her about the meaning of authority. I took her aside and rather straightforwardly, but gently, explained to her that she was mistaken. She came to see it my way. It was a scary moment for a first time father, but the fact is she did not say anything to her daddy that he had not said to his daddy many years before. One way or another (I really can't remember exactly how. Or have I just suppressed the painful memory?) his daddy had also made clear to him the mistaken notion of life without authority.

Generation by generation we must learn and relearn the same lessons – among them are lessons about authority. From our earliest days we have an ingrained, untaught independence. That independence will inevitably come into conflict at some point with authority. It may be with a parent; in fact that is probably the place it will happen first. It may be with a teacher. It could be with a law enforcement officer. Authority, however, is a part of the warp and woof of the universe and God resides behind and above all legitimate authority. If you never learn the lessons of authority and submission in this life, you will ultimately and finally learn them when you stand before him who is the seat of all authority (Phil. 2:9-11).

Children of all ages, whether two or ninety-two, wrestle with the issues of authority. It is part of our fallen human nature. Perhaps what is most frightening to the Christian studied in the Scriptures is to see the world recklessly deifying the fallen human nature of man and its natural bent toward absolute independence.

The resulting chaos is everywhere. The New Age movement. The occult resurgence. The lie that man is inherently good. Broken homes. Fractured relationships. War. Famine. Even the, perhaps well-intentioned, children's rights movement. The secular media is even beginning to ask if perhaps we have not gone too far.

Wherever man struggles with authority and submission, regardless of who and where the particular confrontation is waged, in the final analysis his is a struggle against God. The authority of God is the root issue in all authority struggles. A fight with God may not be in the fore of the person's mind, it may not even be a passing or conscious thought, but the bottom line is that there is only one throne and God is on it. If, even for a moment, we would meet that authority, all our other skirmishes with lesser authorities would be dealt with. Our disgust with delegated authority is removed when we meet direct authority.

That is a radical assertion, I realize. So radical that only people familiar with the Scriptures will buy it without further evidence. Fundamentally our need is to once again gain a clear apprehension and vision of the glory, sovereignty, holiness and authority of God. Sixty-one times in the book of Ezekiel (from chapters 6–39) we read phrases such as 'Then they will know that I am the LORD' (7:27). Ezekiel ministered to the exiled Jewish people in Babylon after they had been removed from their land because of their sin. Peppered on every page of the text are the incessant reminders that fundamentally the need of a fallen people is to see, understand, and appreciate the fullness of who God is. Repentance is needed, yes. But repentance can never be had until there is a new, fresh view of God in his grandeur and beauty.

It is interesting to note the way in which Ezekiel's prophecy opens. Upon opening its pages we happen upon an experience so profound that words nearly fail to describe it. At the opening of his ministry the prophet Ezekiel was granted a vision of the glory of the God he was called to speak for (Ezek. 1–2). Before the world at large will ever see and understand who God is, we in the church must have our vision of the glory and greatness of God restored. The prophet as well as the people must come to grips with the authority of the sovereign Lord.

How, may I ask, does one go about proving the obvious? How does one describe the hand in front of a man's face when he refuses to see it? George Orwell said it well, 'We have now sunk to a depth at which the restatement of the obvious is the first duty of intelligent men.'[1] Bill Hull is right, 'Nothing is so treacherous as the obvious. Like walking a tightrope in a high wind, understanding and executing the obvious is tricky. The obvious restated and applied shakes the church at its foundation.'[2] How then does one go about asserting the absolute authority of God?

We must start by reminding ourselves that, regardless of whether or not it is decided I have done an adequate job in my attempt to put forward the obvious authority of God, God is still the absolute authority of the universe. God's authority is not dependent upon my ability to understand it or explain it.

I believe, for all its difficulty, we can put forward in plain ways the invisible but obvious authority of God. Allow me to give you three words: names, attributes and acts. If you could know what a person's name is, what their nature is like and what they do, you would know the person. So it is with God. The names, attributes and acts of God all testify of his authority.

The *names* or *titles* of God assert at every turn the authority of God. Many generations ago the poet queried, 'What's in a name?' When it comes to the names and titles of God, the answer is 'A great deal!' Herbert Lockyer, in his classic *All the Divine Names and Titles in the Bible*, has taken 341 pages to answer that question.[3] God is called King (Ps. 10:16), Judge (Ps. 50:6), Lord (Ps. 29:20), Master (Jude 1:4), Sovereign (1 Tim. 6:15), God Most High (Ps. 57:2), Almighty (Ps. 93:4), Creator (1 Pet. 4:19), the LORD of Hosts (Ps. 24:10), Shepherd (Ps. 23:1), Father (2 Cor. 6:18), King of kings (Rev. 19:16), and Yahweh (Ps. 20:1).

Among these are the descriptive Hebrew names of God. *El* (the Mighty One) or its plural form *Elohim* is often hyphenated with other Hebrew words to expound upon the nature of God. He is *El Elyon* (God Most High, Gen. 14:18-22), *El-Roi* (The Lord that Sees, Gen. 16:13, 14), *El Olam* (the God of Eternity, Isa. 40:28), *El Shaddai* (The Almighty, Gen. 17:1).

Similarly God is often referred to by the Hebrew word *Yahweh* (often translated Jehovah). *Yahweh* was the name of God most often associated with his covenant relationship with his people. So revered was this name that copyists of the Hebrew scriptures refused to pen or pronounce it. To avoid possible misuse of this holy name of God some have made reference to it by use of euphemisms such as 'The Name', 'The Great and Terrible Name', 'The Peculiar Name', 'The Separate Name', 'The Unutterable Name', 'The Ineffable Name', 'The Incommunicate Name', 'The Holy Name', or 'The Distinguished Name'.[4]

Yahweh was also hyphenated with other Hebrew words to give fuller description of God's character. He is called *Yahweh-Elohim* (The Majestic Omnipotent God, Zech. 13:9), *Yahweh-Hoseenu* (The LORD Our Maker, Ps. 95:6), *Yahweh-Jireh* (The LORD Our Provider, Gen. 22:14), *Yahweh-Rophi* (The LORD Our Healer, Exod. 15:26), *Yahweh-Eloheenu* (The LORD Our God, Deut. 6:4), *Yahweh-Tsebaoth* (The LORD of Hosts, 1 Sam.

1:3), *Yahweh-Tsidkenu* (The LORD Our Righteousness, Jer. 23:5,6), to name just a few.

Many fine studies have been published with a more comprehensive treatment of the names and titles of God than we can give ourselves to here. These few selections, however, reveal the sovereign authority of God. In the Bible an individual's name was often revelatory of their nature and attributes. Never was this more true than with the names of God.

Our second word is *attributes*. An attribute is simply something that is true of God. 'The divine attributes are what we know to be true of God. He does not possess them as qualities; they are how God is as he reveals himself to his creatures.'[5] So what is God like? For one thing, God is self-existent. That is to say that God has the ground of being within himself. God does not depend upon anything. Before anything was, God was – perfect, complete. Were all of creation suddenly to disappear – no more air, earth, water, people, plants, animals, planets or stars – God would remain unaltered in his completeness, undiminished in his perfection. God is also omnipotent. God is able to do anything he wills to do. God is omniscient, he knows all things, past, present and future, instantly from all of eternity, whether those things be what actually happens or only what could potentially happen. We lie awake at night worrying and wondering 'What if?' God knows all the 'What ifs?'! God never learns, discovers or finds out anything. God is omnipresent – he is everywhere present in his creation as a Person. God is sovereign. He alone holds the absolute right to rule and govern his creation according to his good pleasure. God forever holds the reins of the universe in his hands. God is immutable and unchanging. God is not in process. God can not grow. He can not improve. He can not get worse. He is the Lord and he changes not (Mal. 3:6). God is eternal. He has always been. There will never be a time he will not be. God is infinite, that is to say that he knows no boundaries. Imagine every attribute of God pressed to its farthest reaches, then recognize that he is unspeakably beyond even that! God is infinite in his love, grace, forgiveness, mercy, wrath, kindness, holiness, justice, power, knowledge, wisdom, goodness and faithfulness – just to mention a few.

A. W. Tozer's words challenge me.

> What comes into our minds when we think about God is the most important thing about us ... the most portentous fact about any man is not what he at any given time may say or do, but what he in his deep heart conceives God to be like. We tend by a secret law of the soul to move toward our mental image of God.... Were we able to extract from any man a complete answer to the question, 'What comes into your mind when you think about God?' we might predict with certainty the spiritual future of that man.[6]

Yes, God's attributes, along with his names and titles, speak of his absolute authority. To misread what these say to us about him is not a sign of cleverness, but that we are courting disaster.

The *acts* of God also speak to us of his absolute, sovereign authority. What has God done? He spoke a word and things that were not before, now are. Light came at a word from God. Earth, stars, planets, vegetation, human beings all came at the simple articulation of God's Word. The Red Sea split, the Jordan divided, the sun stood still in the sky, fire fell from heaven, lepers were cleansed, paralytics leapt for joy, blind eyes saw. Only One with authority could accomplish such actions.

Do you see the point? If we make any claim to worship the God of the Bible, we must admit that we are coming to One who is absolute in sovereign authority. Why, then, do we so often approach him as if we were coming to an arbitration table? We don't bargain with God. There is no informing him. We cannot polish his plans. At times our prayers sound like a cheapskate bartering with a merchant in a third-world flea market! God is to be submitted to – absolutely, unreservedly.

I find that there are generally two different responses in the face of such facts. One response is the person who says, 'OK, I hear what you are saying. But how do I know it is true?' The other is, 'Fine, but how does this work out in practical terms? Where in the push and shove of life do I encounter this authority of God?' The first is a doubter, the second a seeker. To both I offer two words about the expression of God's authority in this world: revelation and delegation.

The only way we can ever perceive or come into a relationship with God's authority is for him to reveal himself to us. Please understand me – he *is* authority whether or not he ever unveils that authority to us. God is under no obligation to reveal himself to us. He has, however, graciously chosen to uncover something of who he is. According to the degree God has revealed himself to us we stand accountable to him.

How has God revealed himself to us? Where is it we see his authority? We see God in the world around us. Theologians call this 'general revelation'. The Scriptures tell us: 'For since the creation of the world God's invisible qualities – his eternal power and divine nature – have been clearly seen, being understood from what has been made, so that men are without excuse' (Rom. 1:20).

God has also revealed himself through his written Word. Repeatedly the Hebrew prophets proclaimed 'Thus saith the Lord!' 'The lion has roared – who will not fear? The Sovereign Lord has spoken – who can but prophecy?' (Amos 3:8). God has also spoke through the Living Word – Jesus Christ. John said: 'In the beginning was the Word, and the Word was with God, and the Word was God. He was with God in the beginning.... The Word became flesh and made his dwelling among us. We have seen his glory, the glory of the One and Only, who came from the Father, full of grace and truth.... No one has ever seen God, but God the One and Only, who is at the Father's side, has made him known' (John 1:1, 14, 18). This is commonly known as 'special revelation'. Jesus came as One with authority over sin (Luke 5:17-26). He taught with authority (Matt. 7:29). Jesus declared that he had all authority in heaven and on earth (Matt. 28:18). One day every knee will bow and every tongue confess that he is Lord (Phil. 2:9-10). He is declared to be the King of kings and Lord of lords (Rev. 19:16). The final chapter of human history will be one in which the kingdoms of this world will become the Kingdom of our Lord and of his Christ and he will reign forever and ever (Rev. 11:15)!

The world about us, the written Word delivered to us, and the Living Word who walked among us – through all three, with ever-increasing clarity, God has unveiled to mankind his sovereign, over-riding authority. God has not shown us all of himself – as if we could perceive or endure it if he did! What he has shown us of himself should serve to prostrate us before him in humble worship. So as we meet God, in creation but ever more clearly in Scripture and in Christ, we come face to face with the authority of the Ruler of the universe. In that place there can be no objections, no reasoning, no bargaining. The only appropriate response to authority is submission.

One of the most beautiful and powerful expressions of this authority came in the hour of Christ's greatest vulnerability. In the Garden – having been betrayed by a friend, having sweat great drops of blood, having agonized over the cup before him – Jesus with a simple word expressed his authority.

> So Judas came to the grove, guiding a detachment of soldiers and some officials from the chief priests and Pharisees. They were carrying torches, lanterns and weapons. Jesus, knowing all that was going to happen to him, went out and asked them, 'Who is it you want?' 'Jesus of Nazareth,' they replied (John 18:3-5a).

What follows next demonstrates the awesome authority of the One who would give himself for our sins. '"I am he," Jesus said. When Jesus said, "I am he," they drew back and fell to the ground' (18:5b-6). With two simple words (in Greek, literally, 'I am') Jesus drew upon the authority of heaven and manifested his authority on earth. The immediate response of the lesser beings challenging his authority was prostration. With the simple pronouncement that he was the very same God, now in human flesh, who had met with Moses at the burning bush and announced himself as 'I AM' (Exod. 3:14), the mightiest of men were inexplicably thrown to the ground.

> But when he answered, 'I am he,' what was it that so suddenly affected them? Did some stray beams of concealed glory burst forth from their confinement to indicate his majesty?
> Did they dread the putting forth of that power which had been so often exerted to save and bless? We cannot tell. But, whatever the causes, the crowd suddenly fell back in confusion, and were flung to the ground ... the power that sent that rough hireling band reeling backward to the ground could easily have held them there, or plunged them as Korah, Dathan, and Abiram, into living graves.[7]

Some might still complain, 'Fine. That is all well and good, but this whole concept of God's authority is still sort of "out there". It is too ethereal and non-substantive for me. Where, in the world I live in, do I meet up with this authority of God?' This brings us to delegation. In his administration of the universe he has created, God has chosen to delegate some of his authority to various channels within his creation. Using selected vessels of his sovereign choosing, God has determined to execute his authoritative reign of the universe through delegation of measured portions of that authority. Among those to whom God has delegated some measure of his authority are the state (Rom. 13:1-4), the church and its leaders (Heb. 13:17), the home (Eph. 5:22–6:4), and those who believe in him (Eph. 1–2).

We will turn momentarily to examine each of these delegated authorities in detail, but for now we must recognize that as we meet these divinely appointed authorities, we meet God's authority. To be sure none of those listed are perfect. Not all act responsibly with the authority delegated to them.

All are accountable to him who is supreme for their stewardship of his authority. That does not mean that each of these delegated authorities is powerful, but it does mean they are vested with authority.

It is reported that British essayist G. K. Chesterton, during a conversation with fellow writer Alexander Woollcott, explained the relationship of power and authority. As they sipped tea, Chesterton said that if a rhinoceros were to enter the restaurant where they sat, there would be little use in denying he possessed any power. But, Chesterton asserted, he would be the first to rise and assure the chap that he had no authority whatsoever in that place.

Perhaps the classic illustration of the difference between power and authority is that of a policeman who stands in the middle of a busy intersection directing traffic. As he stands there with thousands upon thousands of tons of metal, rubber and plastic thundering down upon him from all directions – he possesses authority. All it takes is the simple motion of an upturned hand and a toot on his whistle and a massive eighteen wheeler squeals to a stop. A flick of the wrist and the Ford station wagon on his left is moved through the intersection. The motorcycle driver behind him waits with eyes fixed upon the officer. That policeman possesses authority. There is little doubt that should the driver of one of even the smallest of vehicles in those lines of traffic decide that he did not have to heed that officer's authority he could run him over. That sports car would have the power to run him down, but not the authority to defy him. Soon the driver of the vehicle would meet with others vested with the same authority the traffic officer had; but this time they would have the power to enforce the authority previously exercised.[8]

Even if we have the power to defy one with delegated authority, we always meet with authority in the end. Power and authority are not the same thing, but God possesses both, absolutely and infinitely. His delegated authorities do not have all power, but God has authorized them to exercise his power and authority in the sphere to which he has assigned them.

Delegated authorities are not God, but they have been appointed to act on God's behalf. Thus, to oppose the one to whom God has delegated his measured authority, is to oppose God. 'The authorities that exist have been established by God. Consequently, he who rebels against the authority is rebelling against what God has instituted, and those who do so will bring judgement on themselves' (Rom. 13:2).

Perhaps no greater illustration of the appreciation for delegated authority exists than David, the man who would become king of Israel. In David's relationship with Saul we observe a healthy view of delegated authority. Saul, of course, was the first king of Israel and David the second. The people of Israel, coming out of the chaos of the period of the judges, called out to God and the prophet Samuel to give them a king, just like all the other nations had (1 Sam. 8:5). This was a rejection of God's authoritative reign over the people (1 Sam. 8:7), but he allowed it and used it to his greater purposes. Soon afterward Saul was anointed by God through Samuel as the first king of the nation (10:1). The citizens of the nation soon ratified this anointing as well (10:24; 11:14-15). This tale of Saul and his people appears to begin to be woven together into a beautiful tapestry, but soon it all begins to unravel. Not long afterward the new king drew the prophet's rebuke (13:11-14). Another blunder followed quickly on the heels of the first (14) and nearly cost the nation the life of the heir-apparent. The final blow came when Saul's rebellion was complete, as we saw in the last chapter. The prophet of God announced, 'You have rejected the word of the LORD, and the LORD has rejected you as king over Israel! ... The LORD has torn the kingdom of Israel from you today and has given it to one of your neighbors' (15:26, 28).

The narrative records God's anointing being conferred upon David as the next king of the people of Israel (16:13). Then ensued the long struggle of an Ichabod-king's last attempts to grasp at power and the patient example of the one anointed to take his place. Though David had been anointed by God to be the next king, it would be a good many years before he ever took the office officially. Some commentators estimate it was at least fourteen years between the time God anointed David as king and the time he actually began to reign over the entire nation.

What is instructive for our purposes is that David never once attempted to establish his own authority. Yes, God's anointing rested upon him. There was another anointed one still on the throne, however. Saul was rebellious, disobedient, and harmful to the nation. But he was, in David's eyes, still God's anointed. David refused to take matters into his own hands to establish his own authority. On two occasions David had opportunity to slay Saul and seize the kingdom that God had declared to be rightfully his (1 Sam. 24, 26). Yet in each instance, though counseled by the men around him to seize the throne, David refused to touch the Lord's anointed (24:6; 26:9).

David's conviction about honoring the one delegated with God's authority was complete. When a young man arrived to announce to David that Saul was dead and reported that he had done David a great favor by putting Saul to death (2 Sam. 1:10), David had him slain for daring to reach out against the Lord's anointed one (1:14-16).

After years of anticipation, Saul, the rejected and rebellious king, was gone and the path to the throne of the nation was clear – right? Was not David God's anointed? Was not David chosen as the one to whom God delegated his authority to lead the nation for him? It was not so simple as that for David. Following Saul's death David inquired of the Lord if he should go up to one of the towns of Judah (2 Sam. 2:1). We wonder aloud, 'Should you go up? David, of course you should! You are anointed by God!' Not only did David inquire as to whether he ought to go up to one of the towns of Judah to lead the nation, he asked which one of the towns he should go to. 'Jerusalem, of course!' would have been our response. God, however, told David to go to Hebron. Why? Because there the tribe of Judah would recognize God's anointing on him and confer upon him their anointing as well (2 Sam. 2:4). Not all the tribes of the nation concurred, however. David waited, again patiently. For over seven years David waited, contented in Hebron though he knew well God's will for him as king of the entire nation. Why did he wait? He waited because in the fracas of Saul's death the other tribes of Israel took Saul's son Ish-Bosheth and anointed him as king in his father's place (2 Sam. 2:8-10). When at last Ish-Bosheth was murdered, David had his assassins put to death for touching the one anointed by the people, just as he had with his father's supposed murderer (2 Sam. 4:9-12).

At long last, many years after God had anointed him king of the nation, 'All the tribes of Israel came to David at Hebron ... and they anointed David king over Israel' (2 Sam. 5:1, 3). Do you see the truth here for us?

> Because David maintained the authority of God, God acknowledged him as a man after his own heart. The kingdom of David continues until now; even the Lord Jesus is a descendant of David. Only those who are subject to authority can be authority. This matter is exceedingly serious. We must eradicate all roots of rebellion from within us. It is absolutely essential that we be subject to authority before we exercise authority.[9]

God is the absolute, unrivaled authority of the universe. This fact is observable through contemplation of the names, nature and actions of God. We encounter God's authority through revelation and delegation. The first comes to us through observation of God's world, and most especially when we contemplate the Living Word of God, Jesus Christ, and his written Word, the Bible. We also daily encounter God's authority as it is delegated in measured form to those whom God has appointed to aid in the administration of his creation.

At every turn we find man revolting against God's authority – whether it is in its undiluted state or delegated through secondary channels. That proclivity toward rebellion has been around since Satan uttered his five fatal 'I will's', culminating with 'I will make myself like the Most High' (Is. 14:13-14). The lie was passed on to Eve – 'you will be like God' (Gen. 3:5) and was soon swallowed by Adam as well. Generation to generation we have handed down the inborn heritage of an aversion to authority.

We dress our rebellion in socially acceptable robes, but at its root it is still the same. We flee through hedonism, believing the lie that satisfaction of the senses is our right and the only path to happiness. We flee God's authority through philosophy, science and education, believing that if we exalt the mind we can finally find our autonomy. Humanism looks like the winding path to freedom, but it is laden with the land mines of self-absorbtion. 'The good life' and 'the American dream' are in many instances only cleverly disguised titles for selfishness. Even religion can be a flight from God's authority – if it is religion ruled by our conventions, consensuses, and customs rather than by him.

Our flight from God's authority is costing us dearly, as we saw in the first chapter. Seldom has the foolishness of our flight from God's authority been put more eloquently than it has been in the dedication page to Dr. Henry Brandt's book *When You're Tired of Treating the Symptoms, And You're Ready For a Cure, Give Me a Call.*[10] The dedication page appears as follows:

The world is self existing....
There is no God....
No deity can save us: we must save ourselves....
Ethics is autonomous and situational,
needing no theological sanction....

As in 1933, humanists still believe that traditional theism, especially faith in the prayer-hearing God, assumed to love and care for persons, to hear and understand their prayers, and to be able to do something about them, is an unproved and outmoded faith.... Reasonable minds look to other means for survival....

HUMANIST MANIFESTO II, 1973

The fool has said in his heart, 'There is no God.'
SOLOMON'S FATHER, 1000 BC (Psalm 14:1, NKJV)

Someone, now anonymous to me, once said, 'If there is anything the non-conformist hates worse than a conformist it's another non-conformist who doesn't conform to the prevailing standard of non-conformity.' So it is. Our world goes on tearing itself apart under the absolute conviction that there are no absolutes. The highest price we pay in this life for the rejection of God's authority may well be the resulting chaos and confusion of this planet we now call home. We appear to be revisiting the days of the Judges when 'everyone did what was right in their own eyes' (Judg. 21:25).

For our own health, individually and corporately, we must come back to the safety of the authority of God. Not in some abstract way, but in obedience to specific commands of God's word that we have been avoiding and in submission to specific delegated authorities in our lives.

Do you suppose that we mature, technologically advanced, scholarly, wise, cultured, progressive adults appear from God's point of view to look much different from that skinny little girl who proudly declared to her daddy: 'I don't have to do what you say!'? The uncomfortable fact is that all of us have a natural bent that lends us to point our finger to the sky and make the same presumptuous statement to the Heavenly Father. Oh, we do it only in the most civil, intellectual and polite of ways of course, but the heart reality is the same.

Isaiah's description of the eighth century people of Judah sounds uncomfortably familiar. 'These are a rebellious people, deceitful children, children unwilling to listen to the LORD's instruction. They say ... to the prophets, "Give us no more visions of what is right! Tell us pleasant things, prophesy illusions. Leave this way, get off this path, and *stop confronting us with the Holy One of Israel!*"' (Isa. 30:10-11, emphasis mine).

39

This indictment needlessly rests upon us, however. The promise of God through Isaiah is also ours: 'In repentance and rest is your salvation, in quietness and trust is your strength' (Isa. 30:15). We must come again under the authority of God. It begins in individual hearts. Will you return to your rest? Jesus is only a prayer away.

NOTES

1. Quoted in Bill Hull, *The Disciple Making Pastor* (Old Tappan, New Jersey: Fleming H. Revell Company, 1988), p.13.

2. Ibid.

3. Herbert Lockyer, *All the Divine Names and Titles in the Bible* (Grand Rapids: Zondervan Publishing House, 1975).

4. Ibid., p.17.

5. A. W. Tozer, *The Knowledge of the Holy* (San Francisco: Harper and Row, 1961), p.17.

6. Ibid., p.1.

7. F. B. Meyer, *The Life of Love* (Old Tappan, New Jersey: Fleming H. Revel Company, 1987), pp.333, 334.

8. John A. MacMillan, *The Authority of the Believer* (Harrisburg, Pennsylvania: Christian Publications, Inc., 1980), pp.12, 13.

9. Watchman Nee, *Spiritual Authority* (New York: Christian Fellowship Publishers, Inc., 1972), p.44.

10. Henry Brandt, *When You're Tired of Treating the Symptoms, and You're Ready for a Cure, Give Me a Call* (Brentwood, Tennessee: Wolgemuth & Hyatt, Publishers, Inc., 1991).

3

The Authority of God and his Word

Hearing and obeying God's voice grows more difficult by the day. Discerning God's still, small voice over the roar of a civilization screaming toward destruction is no easy task.

Allow me to illustrate. I'm a Green Bay Packer fan; I make no apologies about that. After decades of dismal showings, the Packers began an attempt to return to their glory years. With a new general manager and head coach the organization was attempting to turn the frustrated franchise around. They also began negotiating with an all-pro, free-agent defensive end by the name of Reggie White whose contract with the Philadelphia Eagles had just expired. White, it seemed, would be the cornerstone upon which a superior defensive unit could be built. Of course, other teams were seeking to allure Mr. White as well. At one point in the process Reggie, a committed Christian who makes his living in a subculture in which it is hard to stand for your faith in Christ, told the media, 'I'm going to pray about it and try to hear what God wants me to do.' The next day, while the media was seizing upon his recent remarks, Packer's head coach Mike Holmgren told reporters that he had called Reggie White, but got his answering machine. Coach Holmgren, suddenly seeing his opportunity, left a simple message, 'Reggie, this is God. Go to Green Bay!'

I doubt if Reggie White really thought the voice on his answering machine was that of his Savior. Reggie was going through, however, the same thing that many of us go through every day on a different scene. He was trying to discern God's authoritative voice in a chaotic world. In the process we also often get messages trying to tell us what God's will is. They are not always from above.

How does one discern the difference? How can you find God's clear voice of direction in a mixed up world? If we are to live under the authority of God, it is imperative that we are able to discern his will. God's primary avenue for the communication of his will to his people is the written Word of God. God has a good plan for our lives, that plan involves coming under his direct authority and under the delegated authorities he has placed in our lives. How can we cooperate with them if we are unable to receive clear communications from God?

We have no shortage of people claiming to hear God's voice. Do we believe them? Which ones? Why? Why not? How do we know what God wants for our lives?

God has given us an authoritative expression of his will for our lives ... it is found in the Bible. The Scriptures are God's *only* authoritative guide for life. That will preach if I am speaking to the choir, but the culture at large lets forth a big belly laugh at such propositional dogmatism. In an age of relativism the only thing that is absolutely certain is the absence of absolute truth. Unfortunately too many fail to see the logical breakdown in that position. Instead they dress it up with advanced degrees and then stand it up behind the lecterns of renown universities and name it scholarship. Their blindness has grown darker with the help of those seventy-seven scholars who call themselves the Jesus Seminar. They contend that Jesus never said about 80% of the words attributed to him in the four Gospels. Among the claims of Jesus that end up on the office floor of these sizzors-and-paste theologians is Jesus' claim to be Messiah, his prediction of the end of the world, and such events as the last supper. Neither did Jesus say things like 'I am the way and the truth and the life. No one comes to the Father except through Me' (John 14:6).[1] How convenient.

There is, however, a growing sound of an increasing number of unlikely witnesses to Scripture's authority. While making a commencement address, television journalist Ted

Koppel made a remarkable assertion: 'Truth is not a polite tap on the shoulder; it is a howling reproach. What Moses brought down from Mount Sinai were not the Ten Suggestions; they are Commandments. Are, not were. The sheer beauty of the Commandments is that they codify in a handful of words acceptable human behavior, not just for then or now, but for all time.'[2]

Even more surprising was the defence of the Bible by late night talk show host Jay Leno. In 1996 The Tonight Show with Jay Leno welcomed the vile 'shock jock' radio personality Howard Stern. Stern's appearance coincided with his then recently released book. Mr. Stern had reeled off a blue streak of the usual foul fare to come from his mouth. Then came the time to pitch his new book. Stern made the outragcous claim that his was the fastest-selling book in the history of books. To support his declaration he held up a Bible and pronounced, 'The Gideon Company is now putting *my* book in the place of Bibles in hotels.' Leno, now visibly upset, took the Bible and held it up and said, 'Howard, something terrible is going to happen to you.... This book will strike you down as you go down the road. It will go through the windshield and pierce your heart.' Leno went on, 'I am sounding like an evangelist now, but I predict that's what will happen – suddenly, all that is in this book is making perfect sense to me.'[3]

Even among the intelligentsia who reject the Bible's authority there is a slightly growing awareness of the ultimate failure of relativism. In 1991 philosopher Loyal Rue made a presentation at a symposium of the American Association for the Advancement of Science. He began his presentation by outlining the sad state of affairs among us. In typical fashion he upheld the sacred tenant of the secular – that the Bible, with its 'myths' like the Ten Commandments and the story of Jesus' resurrection, could obviously not be believed. Yet he admitted that with the loss of these beliefs our culture is crumbling without a firm foundation for moral responsibility.

His proposal, therefore, was that we must fabricate a 'noble lie' that will provide us with some kind of rationale for moral living. It matters little, Rue said, whether the 'noble lie' be true or not, so long as it convinces us that we ought to live morally. He said, 'The illusion must be so imaginative and so compelling that it can't be resisted. What I mean by the noble lie is one that deceives us, tricks us, compels us beyond self-interest, beyond ego ... that will deceive us into the view that our moral discourse must serve the interests not only of ourselves and each other, but those of the earth as well.'[4]

Ted Koppel, Jay Leno and Loyal Rue are no flaming fundamentalists, but their confession reveals the growing awareness, even in the secular corners of society, that we must have some authoritative basis for guiding our lives. The liberal/ fundamentalist fracas over the inerrancy of the Bible is now largely behind us. Not that anyone on either side has been convinced by the other. It is just that we have found other areas of theology to sharpen our theological knives upon. One no longer hears much debate in the liberal theological circles over the authority of the Bible; we hear instead frantic physicians attempting to diagnose the death-rattle of a culture.

My concern in this chapter will not be an attempt to convince the already unconvinced. My concern is with us who profess to believe in the authority of the Scriptures. Too often our profession does not match our practice. One survey found that half of Protestants polled could not name at least four of the Ten Commandments that Ted Koppel said codify acceptable human behavior. 40% of Protestants say that they never or hardly ever read one of the over five hundred million Bibles in circulation. 63% of Protestants who attend church could not distinguish between the Old and New Testaments.[5] A Gallup Poll revealed that 60% of Americans attend church at least once a month, but of those only 12% read their Bibles.[6] In addition, were one to bring forth statistics to prove it, it could be demonstrated rather convincingly that the moral condition of those who make up the church is, on the average, eloquent proof that we are not living functionally under the authority of the Bible.

Even where believers do turn to the Word it is often seen as little more than a magical charm. 'Quick,' we fumble about, 'I had better "have devotions" so my meeting with the boss goes well this afternoon!' Perhaps the experience of Delma Meal is what many hope for. On May 8, 1994, when Delma went to worship at her Methodist church in Illinois, she had in hand a brand new Bible she had been given that day as a Mother's Day gift. In the course of the service Delma reached for her Bible, which was still in the original clear cellophane wrap. She peeled back the wrapping and thumbed through the Bible. It fell open to a certain place – a place in which six brand new $100 bills were stashed![7] We grab our Bibles up and look for a magical 'word from the Lord' and in so doing often treat it with all the respect of a rabbit's foot. We may not have high hopes of finding a small fortune, but we are often looking for a quick fix to whatever problem presses us that day.

Please don't misunderstand me. God speaks to us from the Bible; he speaks directly to the details of our daily lives. It is God's Word to *us*. But how can I approach the Scriptures in such a way that I don't use it for my ends, but let God use it in me for his ends?

Consider 2 Timothy 3:14-17 as the place to begin. Here we find the last extant written communication of the apostle Paul before his death. Nero was on the throne. His insanity was picking up speed as the amusements used to occupy his depraved mind lost their luster and he looked for more challenging ventures – like actually running the empire. With the increased hands-on involvement of Nero there came growing pressure upon believers in Jesus Christ. Paul warned Timothy that the days just ahead would grow ever darker (3:1-13). Then, beginning in verse 14, the apostle explained how to make sense out of how God wants us to live in this twisted, hell-bent world. His answer? Stand on the Word of God.

Notice again the context. The coming days will grow ever

darker. But mark this: 'There will be terrible times in the last days. People will be lovers of themselves, lovers of money, boastful, proud, abusive, disobedient to their parents, ungrateful, unholy, without love, unforgiving, slanderous, without self control, brutal, not lovers of the good, treacherous, rash, conceited, lovers of pleasure rather than lovers of God – having a form of godliness but denying its power' (3:1-5)

Paul continues on for the next nine verses describing the evil character of the people who will rule in the last days. The apostle's summary is chilling: 'In fact, everyone who wants to live a godly life in Christ Jesus will be persecuted, while evil men and impostors will go from bad to worse, deceiving and being deceived' (vv.12-13). Just one short inhalation away are his next words, 'But as for you ...' (v.14). As you begin to look to God's Word to discern and hear his voice, expect to see a contrast to the world around you. More often than not God's will is going to stand opposed to the standard operating procedure of the world. Sin-laden logic reasons in the opposite direction of God. Expect a contrast between what you find in the world and what you find in the Scriptures. As the sun of a brilliantly lit snow-covered day brings a recoil to the eyes of a man walking out of a dark house, so too for those who first look away from the darkened reason of the world and gaze into the light of God's truth it may take time to adjust to what they see. Be prepared – living according to God's Word will bring a reaction, perhaps a violent reaction from the world. Don't be shocked by the recoil. 'This is the verdict: Light has come into the world, but men loved darkness instead of light because their deeds were evil. Everyone who does evil hates the light, and will not come into the light for fear that his deeds will be exposed' (John 3:19-20).

Coming, then, to the light of God's truth in the Bible, how do we functionally live under its authority? God's words, breathed out through his spokesman, reveal how we may approach the Scripture so we can come under its authority in a practical way.

We must first approach the Scriptures with *faithfulness*. 'But as for you, continue ...' (v.14). The Greek word translated 'continue' carries the sense of abiding, remaining, continuing, dwelling in one place. The exhortation is to 'stay faithfully put' in the truth you have been given by God. In the chaos of the last days there will be a tendency for the righteous to panic. 'Don't!' is Paul's counsel. You may rest assured in the truth which God has delivered to you. What exactly is it that we are to stay put in? 'But as for you, continue in what you have learned and have become convinced of ...' (v.14). Rest in that body of truth delivered to you; repose your soul in the teaching of the Word of God.

It helps us to realize just how real this temptation was for Timothy and his fellow believers at the time of Paul's writings. What would later become the full-blown heresy of Gnosticism was in its germinal stages in the closing years of the New Testament writers. The primary draw of Gnosticism was that it offered 'gnosis', or wisdom. 'Yes, yes, Christianity is fine,' they would say, 'but if you *really* want to know God, come visit us!' Mingled in an unholy alliance with Christianity, Gnosticism offered a short cut to the deep things of God.

Times have not changed. Everywhere we turn it seems someone is touting a 'new truth'. With the mainline acceptance of the New Age, with the resurgence of the occult, with openness to whatever 'works' to help with our pain and confusion; people run with abandon after every slick religious sales person. God says, 'You already have it! Remain in it!' That is not to say that we have learned all there is to know. The Bible is an inexhaustible supply of truth that we will spend eternity plumbing the depths of. It is to say, however, that all we need to know is in the Book. All the essentials of our faith and life are set before us here in the holy Scriptures.

Every so often there comes to the fore of public attention someone with a 'new' truth from God. Their passion runs deep. Their sincerity is convincing in its own right. They insist that what they have discovered is the key to everything you need. Call me a skeptic if you like, but I am suspicious of some 'new' truth that is sold as essential. I wonder, 'How did the saints over the last two thousand years do without it?' How did Augustine get along without this recent revelation? I wonder how Martin Luther managed to turn the corner in the Reformation without it? How did the nearly innumerable Chinese believers who suffered in the Boxer Rebellion endure without the knowledge of this latest theological invention?

Scripture speaks clearly on this matter of staying faithfully put in the revealed truth of God's Word. 'I write to you, young men, because you are strong, and the word of God lives in you, and you have overcome the evil one' (1 John 2:14b). 'Do not let anyone who delights in false humility and the worship of angels disqualify you for the prize. Such a person goes into great detail about what he has seen, and his unspiritual mind puffs him up with idle notions' (Col. 2:18). 'Do not go beyond what is written' (1 Cor. 4:6). 'I warn everyone who hears the words of the prophecy of this book: If anyone adds anything to them, God will add to him the plagues described in this book' (Rev. 22:18a).

If we are to functionally come under the authority of God and his Word, we must come and keep coming faithfully to the Scriptures as the only infallible and inerrant guide to truth. Too often we come to God as we come to a vending machine. We put in our one or two weeks of sincere effort at reading the Bible and when we don't get the results we want, we bang around for a while trying to manipulate God into answering us on our terms. Finally we abandon the process and shuffle away muttering something about 'I guess it doesn't work for me.' We would all do well to emulate Billy Graham in his early commitment to the Bible. Faced with many doubts and questions about the Bible, as a young minister he prayed, 'Lord, many things in this Book I do not understand. But you have said, "The just shall live by faith." All I have received from you I have taken by faith. Here and now I accept the Bible as your Word. I take it all. I take it all without reservation.

Where there are things I cannot understand, I will reserve judgement until I receive more light. If this pleases you, give me authority as I proclaim your Word and through that authority convict men and women of sin and turn sinners to the Savior.'[8]

Do you suppose God has honored Billy Graham's faithful approach to the Scriptures? Has God guided Mr. Graham through the years? Has God given him wisdom? Has Billy's request for authority in preaching and souls being saved been answered? Remember, the first approach to the Word of God is always to come in faithfulness.

We must also approach the Scriptures with *conviction*. The things that we are to continue in are the things we 'have learned and become convinced of' (v.14). Timothy came to the Word of God, stayed there and immersed himself in it. He learned and became convinced of it. A person may learn, in the sense of collecting data, and yet never allow that learning to solidify into conviction. On the other hand a person may have convictions, but never have really learned anything. The first is knowledgeable, but not wise. The second is simply obnoxious. One is a useless exercise of the mind, the other ignorant foolishness.

We must both learn facts and form convictions. To come under the Scripture's authority we must dig, work hard and labour to learn its truths, understand its doctrines, and digest its principles. We must, through all of that hard effort, keep our own heart very close to the edge of the 'Sword' (Eph. 6:17). We must make certain the truths we digest are converted into the muscle of personal convictions that give us strength to walk in God's ways. Paul has just warned of the kind of people who are 'always learning, but never able to acknowledge the truth' (v.7).

Along with faithfulness and conviction, we must also approach the Scripture with *reflection* if we are to live under its authority. The rationale is given by the apostle: 'because you know those from whom you learned it, and how from infancy you have known the holy Scriptures, which are able to make you wise for salvation through faith in Christ Jesus' (v.14b-15). To whom is Paul referring? Earlier in this letter Paul has made clear the identity of those to whom he makes reference here. 'I have been reminded of your sincere faith, which first dwelt in your grandmother Lois and in your mother Eunice and, I am persuaded, now lives in you also' (1:5).

In the midst of discussing the confusion of the last days and how to stand firm on the authority of the Word of God, Paul added this exhortation to personal reflection upon the lives of those who have imparted the Word of God to him. It would seem that Timothy's father was probably a Gentile and an unbeliever, while his mother was a believing Jew (Acts 16:1). It does not take a great deal of imagination to picture the rough time Eunice may have had raising her son for Jesus Christ and instilling biblical values in him. Single mothers and ladies with unsaved husbands, be encouraged!

I believe, however, that Paul is not only referring to his mother and grandmother, but in an indirect way to himself as well. Timothy was eager in ministry for Christ when Paul found him. Timothy traveled as Paul's personal traveling companion and co-laborer in the ministry during his second and third missionary journeys. Oh, how many learning opportunities that must have afforded Timothy! His was a biblical education of not only content, but of life, method, and manner as well. If we are to live under the authority of God's Word we must have those select individuals in our lives to whom we are willing to attach ourselves and be mentored. We need a person close enough to us, who knows us intimately enough, who loves us deeply enough to instill the Scriptures in us and make clear, even painfully clear, the implications of what we have read and studied. 'Remember your leaders, who spoke the word of God to you. Consider the outcome of their way of life and imitate their faith' (Heb. 13:7).

We must reflect directly upon the Word of God, and also on the lives of faithful people who live out that Word. Be it mother, grandmother, or spiritual mentor we all need the living, breathing illustration of the truths of Scripture that gets up on two legs and walks down the path of life with us. There is great advantage, for the person who seeks to live under the authority of Scripture, in having such a friend and spiritual mentor.

The mentor who has fulfiled this role in my life to this point, perhaps more than any other, was my pastor throughout my high school and college years. He found me a shy, easily intimidated adolescent. Yet he began to befriend me, teach me, guide me, teach me, show me, teach me, challenge me, teach me, let me try it, teach me – all the while affirming that he loved me. Humanly speaking, I would not be walking with Christ, let alone serving him as I am, if it were not for a humble, faithful man named Allen Sparks. Allen, by his own admission, is not a man of flash, glitz or pizazz. He is, however, full of one indispensable quality – faithfulness. I for one want to rise up and bless God for him. When I come to live under the authority of God's Word I often think back on Allen Sparks. I am too prone to ignore my blind spots. Allen was never polite enough to leave my blind spots alone. I am too prone to protect my own comfort. Allen was never socially conscious enough to keep from disrupting my comfort zone if it could mean spiritual benefit for me. I need Allen and I need others like him in my life. You do too, if you are going to live under the authority of the Word of God, because the authority of God's Word is not complete until the learning becomes conviction. I had never heard the word 'conviction' until I met Allen Sparks.

We must come to Scripture with faithfulness, conviction and reflection. We must also approach the Scriptures with *reverence* if its authority is to rule in our lives. 'All Scripture is God-breathed ...', said the apostle (v.16a). When we hold a Bible in our hands we are handling something that has its origin in God himself. Where else in our lives do we hold, touch, and handle something concrete that has its origin directly from God? E. J. Young's comments put us on the right track:

Why did Paul thus speak of the Scriptures? he thus spoke, we believe, because he wished to make as clear as possible the fact that the Scriptures did not find their origin in man but in God. It was God the Holy Ghost who breathed them forth; they owed their origin to him; they were the product of the creative breath of God himself. It is a strong figure, this expression 'breathed out by God.' A strong figure, however, is needed, in order that Timothy may realize that he is being asked to place his confidence not in writings which merely express the hopes and aspirations of the best of men, but rather in writings which are themselves actually breathed out by God, and consequently of absolute authority.[9]

Someone argues, however, 'But my translation varies from yours. With all the translations and interpretations how can I really say that I am holding God's Word in my hand?' Notice that these very words were just referred to by the apostle as 'the holy Scriptures' (v.15), a virtual technical term for the Septuagint or Greek translation of the Old Testament. When Paul or Timothy held in their hands a copy of the Greek translation of the Old Testament they knew them to be the very words of God breathed out for them. Thus they approached those Scriptures reverently.

Once we understand the divine origin of the Scriptures we approach them reverently and thus are able to wield them powerfully. Did not Jesus himself, when tempted by the devil, confidently hold forth the words of God as his weapon (Matt. 4:1-11)? When Satan attempted to entice Jesus to believe he needed something more than God's truth, Jesus asserted that 'Man does not live on bread alone, but on every word that comes *from the mouth of God*' (Matt. 4:4, emphasis mine). Jesus, understanding the divine origin of the Scriptures, used their authority and the evil one recoiled.

The church, throughout the ages, has understood the divine origin of the Scriptures. A proper understanding of their origin led to a reverence of their nature that in turn issued forth in power to the one who first came under their authority and then declared them in Jesus' name. There was Irenaeus in the second century who called us to be, 'Most properly assured that the Scriptures are indeed perfect, since they were spoken by the word of God and his Spirit.' In the fourth century Cyril of Jerusalem declared, 'We must not deliver anything whatsoever, without the sacred Scriptures, nor let ourselves be misled by mere probability, or by marshaling of arguments. For this salvation of ours by faith is ... by proof from the sacred Scriptures.' Augustine said, 'I have learned to hold the Scriptures alone inerrant.' Luther wrote, 'The Scriptures, although they also were written by men, are not of men nor from men, but from God.' Again he said, 'We must make a great difference between God's Word and the word of man. A man's word is a little sound, that flies into the air, and soon vanishes; but the Word of God is greater than heaven and earth, yea, greater than death and hell, for it forms part of the power of God, and endures everlastingly.' John Calvin similarly said: 'This is a principle which distinguishes ours from all others, that we know that God has spoken to us ... We owe to the Scripture the same reverence which we owe to God; because it has proceeded from him alone, and has nothing belonging to man mixed with it.' R. A. Torrey affirmed, 'The Bible is the Word of God. The voice that speaks to us from this Book is the voice of God.'[10]

In his Word we encounter the divinely given expression of his authoritative will for man. It cannot be improved upon. The Scriptures do not need our help. The Scriptures call us to bow before the God who breathed them out. We are not worshipers of the Bible, but of the God whose Word it is! Truly the Bible is unlike any other book. When we approach the Scriptures with this kind of appropriate reverence there will be an expectancy in our reading and study. God will honour his Word when we accept it for what it is, the very words of God himself to those he loves.

Perhaps it would seem that if we approach the Scriptures reverently it should go without saying that we will approach them with *teachability* also. How many times have we come to the Bible and prayed, 'Lord, give me a blessing'? Or we come to the Bible attempting to find a verse to placard above plans already devised and committed to? How often do we approach Scripture for confirmation of what we want to do, rather than discovery of what God wants us to do? Even further yet, it is infinitely harder to avoid the 'What do you want me to do?' approach to Scripture until we have first asked, 'What do you want me to *be*, Lord?'

The Scriptures, Paul said, are 'useful for teaching, rebuking, correcting and training in righteousness, so that the man of God may be thoroughly equipped for every good work' (v.16b-17). There is a fourfold purpose for Scripture in our lives. The Bible is to teach us – to impart knowledge we do not have naturally and can find nowhere else. It is to reprove us – to lay a straightedge next to our confused and twisted ways of thinking and behaving. The Scriptures are to correct us – to call us back to God's pathway when we have meandered after our own best ideas. The Bible is also to train us. The word here comes from the root meaning 'child' and thus is often used in reference to the rearing of a child into adulthood. The element of discipline is prominent in its meaning.[11] Indeed we meet the word again in the classic passage on God's discipline of his children: 'My son do not make light of the Lord's discipline, and do not lose heart when he rebukes you, because the Lord disciplines those he loves' (Heb. 12:5-6a).

If we are to live practically under the authority of God we must come to it and thoroughly digest its truths, facts, structure, persons, books, events, themes and doctrines. In short, we must allow it to instruct us. Diligent, sweat-laden toil in study must be ours if we are to truly abide under the authority of Scripture (1 Tim. 4:15). God's Word is to instruct us, but it will never do so apart from our disciplined, consistent, hard work of study.

We must allow the Word to personally rebuke us if we are to truly come under its authority. We must allow God, through the Scriptures, to reprove us. No opinion, no pet doctrine, no viewpoint can be so cherished that it is not brought under the white-hot light of God's truth. In God's gracious plan for us he uses others of his people, graciously holding the Word of God before us, to lay bare half-truths in our thinking. We are, unfortunately, impervious to our blind spots. Thankfully God will not let us rest in that state. Who is there in your life that can challenge you at your most sensitive and vulnerable places, and you will truly listen? If we do not have at least several such people, we may not be living under the authority of God's Word.

As difficult as it is to see the error of our thinking, God's Word serves not only the negative function of pointing out error, but it also serves the positive intention of correcting us. It enables us to come back to the right path after having wandered away. We are not only taken up short when wrong, but empowered to come back to the right. How practical do you get when it comes to the application of what you read each day in God's Word? Sir Thomas Beecham once said, 'If an opera cannot be played by an organ grinder it is not going to achieve immortality.'[12] Scripture is classic, we must approach it reverently. But it is for common people like you and me. We are the organ grinders of the world, plain ordinary folks. There is, however, a divine Word for us that plays as well in our 'daily grind' as in the lofty towers of the most eminent theologians. We must, however, become persistently practical in its application.

How has God's Word disciplined you lately? We are all children under God the Father's tutelage. Our Father's favourite means of training us is his own Word. Using a different metaphor, Jesus made the same point to the disciples: 'I am the true vine, and my Father is the gardener. He cuts off every branch in me that bears no fruit, while every branch that does bear fruit he prunes so that it will be even more fruitful' (John 15:1-2). The Father's intention is that each branch bears, not only fruit, but more fruit. The method of making us more fruitful is to apply the edge of the pruning knife to our lives. God delights when his people bear fruit, but his delight should not be interpreted as final satisfaction. In order that we might be more fruitful he will prune our lives. How does he do so? 'You are already clean because of the word I have spoken to you' (v.3). The word 'clean' in verse three is the same root word as 'prunes' in verse two. The disciples, Jesus said, were already 'pruned' and ready for more fruitfulness than they had to that point experienced. How had they been 'pruned'? The edge of the pruning knife, 'the sword of the Spirit, which is the word of God' (Eph. 6:17), had been laid to their lives as Jesus imparted his Word to them. God's choice instrument in disciplining our lives for fruitful service is his Word. He delights when his people willingly come to his Word, study it, apply it and allow him to prune and discipline them by it. That is painful and many people run from it. God may use other means to discipline our lives, but his instrument of choice is his Word.

Are you teachable as you come to the written Word of God? Will you do the hard thing that God shows you from Scripture? Or do you explain it away, rationalize it, let your mind drift to other people to whom it may apply more? J. B. Phillip's translation drives the point home when he says that God's Word 'is useful for teaching the faith and correcting error, for re-setting the direction of a man's life and training him in good living'.[13] Are you in the Word? Is the Word in you? How you answer those questions answers whether or not you are living functionally under its authority.

Why endure such difficult work? Why subject yourself to it in the first place? It is 'so that the man of God may be thoroughly equipped for every good work' (v.17). 'Thoroughly equipped,' that is the goal. The word translated 'thoroughly' means fit, complete, capable, sufficient, or in other words 'able to meet all demands'.[14] Similarly, 'equipped' means completely outfitted, fully furnished, fully equipped, or fully supplied. The word, in fact, was used in other ancient writings to describe a wagon or a rescue boat that was completely outfitted with all that was necessary for the task at hand.[15]

Recently I did a daring thing, at least by my standards. I went parasailing on the Gulf of Mexico. I had determined ahead of time that I would go through with it, which was important because by the time I was getting into the speedboat to go to the launch site I was having second thoughts. As we were speeding our way along to the site at which I was to go airborne, I noticed that the first mate was training a rookie for his job, which did not build my confidence! Step by step, item by item, the first mate carefully showed the trainee everything needed – every clamp, every fold of the parachute, every motion, every contingency. In short he was making certain that he was 'thoroughly equipped' for what lay ahead. I, for one, was sincerely grateful for the thoroughness and completeness of the training that young man was receiving. I became even more appreciative as I dangled at the end of a thin rope at 1000 feet in the air in a high wind with nothing but open water over my shoulder.

All the preparation has to happen beforehand. If a problem arose at 1000 feet it would have been too late for a look at the training manual. The 'thoroughly equipped' person has paid their dues and toiled somewhere out of the glare of the spotlight. We have become so need-oriented as a society that rarely will we commit energy or attention to anything that we don't feel the need for at the moment. Whatever we 'feel' is what we go after. If I don't feel like that Sunday School class or Bible study is scratching my immediate itch, chances are I won't go back. If we are truly children of this age and we have other more immediate pressures upon us, we likely won't read and study our Bibles on a given day. Yet what are we to do when the need arises and we have not prepared? 'But solid food is for the mature, who *by constant use have trained themselves* to distinguish good from evil' (Heb. 5:14, emphasis mine).

How do we hear God's voice over the roar of a world spinning out of control? Better yet, how do we live under the authority of that voice once we hear it? We must begin by approaching God's Word with faithfulness, conviction, reflection, reverence and teachability.

In a world filled with people hell-bent on living under no one's authority but their own, we have a difficult assignment in trying to live under the authority of God. The screaming of those trying to drown out the sound of God's truth revealed in his Word can make it difficult to hear his voice.

You and I likely do not have a 'message from God' left on our answering machine like Reggie White, but we have many voices telling us how to live. How do we hear God's voice? Turn to his Word! The clear, objective expression of his authoritative will for our lives is given to us there. Are you doing so? Regularly? Intentionally? Passionately?

NOTES

1. 'Scholars credit holy ghostwriter,' Sheboygan Press, Sheboygan, Wisconsin, Sunday, December 12, 1993.

2. Ted Koppel, *Religion and Society Report* 5, 1 (January 1988), 3.

3. A. Larry Ross, 'Tonight Show Prophecy' *Christianity Today*, February 5, 1996, p.13.

4. Quoted in Ravi Zacharias, *Deliver Us From Evil* (Waco, Texas: Word Publishers, 1996), pp. 216-217.

5. Martin E. Marty, quoted in David L. Larsen, *The Anatomy of Preaching* (Grand Rapids: Baker Book House, 1989), p.38.

6. Information provided by Hosanna Ministries, 2421 Aztec Road NE, Albuquerque, NM, 87107-4200.

7. As reported on WFRV TV5, Green Bay, Wisconsin on their 10:00 p.m. News on May 9, 1994.

8. Billy Graham, 'Biblical Authority in Evangelism,' *Christianity Today* 1, 1 (1956): 5-6.

9. Edward J. Young, *Thy Word Is Truth* (Grand Rapids: William B. Eerdmans Publishing Company, 1957), pp.20-21.

10. All quoted from James Montgomery Boice, *Does Inerrancy Matter?* (Oakland: International Council on biblical Inerrancy, 1979), pp.17-20.

11. Ralph Earle, '2 Timothy', in *The Expositor's Bible Commentary*, v.11 (Grand Rapids: Zondervan Publishing House, 1978), p.410.

12. Lawrence J. Peters, *Peter's Quotations* (New York: William Morrow and Company, Inc., 1977), p.341.

13. J. B. Phillips, *The New Testament in Modern English* (New York: Macmillan Publishing Company, 1972).

14. Fritz Reinecker, *A Linguistic Key to the Greek New Testament* (Grand Rapids: Zondervan Publishing House, 1976), p.647.

15. Ibid.

4

The Authority of God and the Government

How should committed followers of Jesus Christ respond to the government under which they live? What if that government is corrupt? Should their response differ if the leaders bless themselves extravagantly out of the government coffers? What if their tax dollars are used for immoral purposes? Is resistance or even rebellion ever permissible? If so, what cues indicate that such a time has come? The ultimate question seems to be, how can one live absolutely under the authority of God and still live under the delegated authority of a government that may not honor him?

These are just the beginning of the tough questions believers must face today. The time is long past when we may deal with them in any abstract, theoretical way. Our answers and our application must be painfully personal.

There is no question that the condition of the United States of America and other Western nations is of great concern to those who love God. Morally we appear to be floundering in the demise of decency. Ethically we seem to have thrown off all boundaries. How are we to respond? When do we 'obey God, rather than men'? Over what issues do we take our stand? What is to be the church's relationship to and mission toward society at large?

If we name the Name of Christ, we must learn to rightly respond to those he has placed in governing authority over us. Romans 13:1-7 is the New Testament's most comprehensive word concerning the responsibility of the believer to the state:

Everyone must submit himself to the governing authorities, for there is no authority except that which God has established. The authorities that exist have been established by God.

Consequently, he who rebels against the authority is rebelling against what God has instituted, and those who do so will bring judgment on themselves. For rulers hold no terror for those who do right, but for those who do wrong. Do you want to be free from fear of the one in authority? Then do what is right and he will commend you. For he is God's servant to do you good. But if you do wrong, be afraid, for he does not bear the sword for nothing. He is God's servant, an agent of wrath to bring punishment on the wrongdoer.

Therefore, it is necessary to submit to the authorities, not only because of possible punishment but also because of conscience.

This is also why you pay taxes, for the authorities are God's servants, who give their full time to governing. Give everyone what you owe him: If you owe taxes, pay taxes; if revenue, then revenue; if respect, then respect; if honor, then honor.

Exegetically, the passage before us is not complicated. The principles are arrived at comparatively easily. The application of them, on the other hand, can be personally painful and mired in controversy. Allow me, for the moment, to simply state several of the basic principles that arise from this passage and then we will take them up individually in more detail. At least four basic principles arise from these words breathed out by God. First, our submission to governing authorities is not optional (v.1a). Second, God establishes every governing authority (v.1b). Third, resisting a governing authority is resisting God (v.2). Finally, God uses the existing governing authorities as tools to achieve our good and his greatest glory (v.3-4).

Anyone who has had to grapple with the realities of sometimes conflicting allegiances of God and of human government realizes how difficult these principles are to put into action. They raise some bewildering questions. Paul appears to be too blanketly dogmatic. The first question that arises is 'always?'. Consider again the first principle given to us in Romans 13:1: our submission to governing authorities is not optional. We respond with great emotion – 'always?' In the face of such biblical teaching some conclude: 'Obviously Paul didn't understand! It is clear that Paul never saw days like ours!' Too many, upon reading such uncomfortable words, simply assume 'Paul just doesn't get it. Paul just didn't live long enough to get a real grip on the topic he is speaking to.' Such reasoning reveals our ignorance first of church history and then of the nature of Scripture.

Did Paul understand what it is to live under a governing authority that did not honor God and that made life difficult? Did he conceive of what he was saying when he said, 'Everyone must submit himself to the governing authorities'? Absolutely. Paul wrote this letter to Roman Christians under the reign of an emperor named Nero. Perhaps you have heard of him, he is rather renowned. He came to the throne at age seventeen and for the first eight years of his reign the empire did well under his 'leadership'. I put 'leadership' in quotation marks because for the first part of his reign Nero actually had little to do with running the empire. Instead he busied himself with racing chariots and singing in musicals, leaving the day by day business of running the empire to his advisors. There came a day, unfortunately, when Nero determined to take a more hands-on approach to government. As he seized more and more control, Nero became increasingly brutal, insane, and immoral in his ways. Nero began to drain the treasury through his elaborate schemes and when he felt the pinch he did what many rulers do, he raised taxes. At one point in the reign of Nero, his mother, Agrippina, began to try to manipulate more and more control over the empire. Frustrated in her efforts, she backed her son's cousin Britannicus. Nero, to secure his position, had Britannicus poisoned to death and his mother banished to exile. He shipped his mother off on a vessel which was designed to sink and kill her, but the plan failed. Thus, in AD 59, Nero called for his mother's return and then had her executed for treason. It is said that he had her abdomen laid open that he might look upon the womb that bore him. In AD 64 riots broke out resulting in much of the city of Rome being burned to the ground. Reportedly Nero actually had set the fire, but in order to divert attention away from himself he blamed the inferno on the Christians. This began the severest of his persecutions upon the believers in Jesus Christ. Nero was known for throwing Christians to the lions and for impaling them upon high stakes and setting them on fire that they might serve as torches to light up his royal gardens at night.[1]

Yes, Paul knew what it was to live under difficult governing authorities. Paul knew the score, and he still wrote Romans 13:1-7! Someone who has checked their calendar, may quickly object and say, 'Paul wrote Romans 13 before Nero really got that bad.' However, Paul wrote Titus much later and said there (3:1-2) virtually the same things. The apostle Peter, on the very eve of Nero's great persecution, wrote the very same commands (1 Pet. 3:13-17).

Even if one continues to demand that Paul didn't know how bad things would get under Nero, one has to admit that he did have knowledge of the Babylonians and Assyrians, both of whom God raised up to discipline his people, Israel. The historical records reveal that the Babylonian and Assyrian kings were among the most vile, cruel, brutal and wicked rulers that ever existed. Yet the Scriptures declare that God raised them to the place of authority.

Paul knew about Herod the Great, a violent, bloody, selfish man. A man who in his paranoia, at the age of seventy, dying of disease and knowing he had been such a vile ruler, did not want the Jewish people to celebrate at word of his death. To avoid the celebration Herod had scores of Jews gathered into the Hippodrome, then he ordered his family to have them all slain when they received word of his death. In this way the Jewish people would not commemorate his death with a party, but rather would go into mourning. Paul, likewise, knew of Archelaus, who had three thousand possible revolutionaries slain. The apostle certainly knew of his brutality toward the Jewish and Samaritan people. He also knew about Herod Antipas, who had John the Baptist beheaded. Paul knew how Pilate had been a governing authority who had himself been ruled by corruption and expediency, not justice. He knew of King Agrippa I, who lived an extravagant, careless life. Paul knew about how he had been behind the early persecution of the church (Acts 12:1-19), even having James killed and Peter and John imprisoned, just to score points with the Jewish people. Paul knew how God cut Agrippa I down in his pride (Acts 12:20-23). Paul was aware of King Agrippa II, whose incestuous relationship with his sister Berenice was the talk of Rome. Paul himself had been beaten and mistreated by various Roman officials (Acts 16:22ff; 2 Cor. 11:25ff).

Let's face it, Paul knew all about immoral, corrupt, debauched, violent, profane, unscrupulous, degenerate governing authorities. Truly, 'When the righteous are in authority, the people rejoice; But when a wicked man rules, the people groan' (Prov. 29:2, NKJV). Yet he chose to pen holy Scripture that states that submission to governing authorities is not optional. Does God's principle, that the submission of his people to their governing authorities is never an option, always stand true? Yes, always.

Let's consider, then, our second principle: God establishes every governing authority. Is this true? Is this *always* true? Many assume that this cannot be true without exception. The skeptic reasons, 'Somewhere, some time in the history of humanity, someone slipped up to the throne of some backwater, third world country that God did not put there.' Our minds rifle through the infamous leaders of history and we wonder to ourselves, 'Him!? Did God truly arrange things so that that person would end up in control?' Yet God's Word stands clear to this day, 'there is no authority except that which God has established. The authorities that exist have been established by God' (Rom. 13:1b). Is this always true? Ask Paul. Remember the rulers in and around his lifetime? These men put some of the men that come to our mind to shame for their mild ways. Paul says that all of these men were there because of God's sovereign choice. This does not mean that any of these men loved God, obeyed God, or were sympathetic to God's cause. They were antithetical to the goodness, holiness and righteousness of God. They dishonored God and they will pay the price of his retribution for their rebellion. Nevertheless, God lifted them to the throne for a time to fulfill a purpose in the outworking of his grand plan.

Does God establish every governing authority – always? Consider one example, that of Cyrus, king of Persia. Cyrus was a pagan king of an ungodly empire. Yet God said of him 'he is my shepherd' and that he 'will accomplish all that I please' (Isa. 44:28), particularly in regard to his people Israel. God called Cyrus 'My anointed', or as we might translate it more literally, 'My messiah' (45:1)! Amazingly this is the same designation God used to mark out the first two kings he had given to Israel, Saul and David (1 Sam. 10:1; 16:6). Notice how both before this section in Isaiah (41:4; 42:8; 43:3, 10, 11-13, 15, 25; 44:6, 8, 24-28) and after it (45:5, 6, 14, 18, 21-23; 46:4, 9) God makes explicit the fact of his absolute sovereign authority over all things. The kingdom to be displaced by Persia was Babylon. Babylon itself had been raised up by God to accomplish his will. The Babylonians, however, grew prideful, even taking for themselves the very statements God had just been making about himself with regard to his sovereign authority (Isa. 47:8, 10) and God called his people to look at how he would punish them (47:9, 11ff). Indeed, God would raise up Persia to discipline, judge and remove the Babylonians. Once again God called Cyrus his 'chosen ally' (Isa. 48:14-15)!

Consider also the pagan king of Babylon whom history has revealed to have been a ruthless and cruel dictator. God calls him, 'my servant Nebuchadnezzar king of Babylon' (Jer. 25:9; 27:6). God chose Nebuchadnezzar to bring horrifying judgement upon his people (25:9-11). Despite the terrifying nature of

Nebuchadnezzar's reign, anyone who spoke against this king was said to have 'preached rebellion against the LORD' (28:16).

Does God always establish every governing authority? Yes. Do we always understand why God does so? No. Are we guaranteed we will understand his purposes in this life? No. God is under no compulsion to bow to the standard of our intelligence. God is sovereign – we sing about it, preach about it, pray about it, teach about it, talk about it – but do we believe it? 'Our God is in heaven; he does whatever pleases him' (Ps. 115:3).

Consider again the third principle that has arisen from Romans 13: Resisting a governing authority is resisting God. Is this always true? Paul said, 'Consequently, he who rebels against the authority is rebelling against what God has instituted, and those who do so will bring judgement on themselves' (Rom. 13:2). Did Paul, however, intend that to be accepted as a universally true statement? Those familiar with the Scriptures turn quickly to Acts 5:29 and remind us of Peter and the apostles who, when ordered by the Jewish ruling authorities not to preach any longer in Jesus' name, declared, 'We must obey God rather than men!' (see also Acts 4:19). Is it always true that resisting a governing authority is resisting God? The answer is no, not always. That quenches our dissatisfaction just long enough to realize another, equally difficult question follows on the heels of this answer. The question is this: When is it permissible (perhaps even required) for believers in Jesus Christ to resist those placed by God as delegated governmental authorities over them? We must give exceedingly great care to answering that question correctly because to answer it wrongly is to risk aligning ourselves against the sovereign authority of God Most High.

When is it permissible, or even mandatory, for believers to disobey the governing authorities placed over them? Notice the following Scriptural examples of people who resisted the governing authorities placed by God over them and who were commended or rewarded for their stand. I list them along with the Scriptures so you can study them in more detail than we have room here to describe.

* The disobedience of the Hebrew midwives and Moses' mother when ordered to put the male Hebrew infants to death (Exod. 1:15–2:10).
* The disobedience of Moses and the Israelites to Pharaoh at the Exodus (Exod. 7–12).
* The refusal of Obadiah to slay the prophets of the Lord at the command of wicked Queen Jezebel (1 Kgs. 18:4).
* The refusal of Shadrach, Meshach and Abednego to bow in worship of the idolatrous image set up by King Nebuchadnezzar of Babylon (Dan. 3).
* The disobedience of Daniel the prophet when he refused to stop praying to the Lord as ordered by King Darius (Dan. 6).
* The instance of Joseph taking Mary and baby Jesus and fleeing into Egypt from Herod when he was attempting to murder all the baby boys in Bethlehem (Matt. 2:13-18).
* The refusal of the apostles when ordered by the Jewish rulers to stop preaching in the Name of Jesus (Acts 4:19; 5:28).
* The refusal of people in the Tribulation period to worship the Antichrist (Rev. 13).

We must determine the common denominator in each of those instances when the people of God refused obedience to the governing authorities over them. What is it which binds these varied events together as similar? It is that, in each case, the people of God disobeyed when they were *compelled* to do something wrong.[2]

When is it permissible to violate God's standard operating procedure of submissive obedience to the governing authorities? Based upon the biblical examples given to us the time for disobedience to governing authorities is not when they pass an unjust law that we do not like. It is not when sin, immorality or wrong is condoned by those who should lead more righteously. It is not when monies collected through taxation from the people are spent in ways that offend the moral convictions of those who believe in Christ. It is not when the country is beginning to head in a direction that believers do not appreciate. It is not even when injustice is perpetrated by those placed in positions of delegated authority by God to dispense justice. The time when it is permissible for God's people to disobey the civil authorities is when they are *compelled* by those authorities to do something that is clearly against the will of God.

This is a hard word for us to hear. Such a response flies in the face of all that is natural to us. I would suggest to you that in all of those instances where biblical characters disobeyed the governing authorities and were commended for it, they continued to submit even though they were unable to obey. We must come to understand the difference between submission and obedience. Normally submission and obedience come to us as subtly distinct, but indivisibly joined. But there are times when you can and must submit to a person placed in authority over you by God and yet not obey him. Perhaps Watchman Nee has stated it best.

Submission is a matter of attitude, while obedience is a matter of conduct.... Obedience, however, cannot be absolute.... Submission ought to be absolute.... When delegated authority (men who represent God's authority) and direct authority (God himself) are in conflict, one can render submission but not obedience to the delegated authority. Let us summarize this under three points:

1. Obedience is related to conduct: it is relative. Submission is related to heart attitude: it is absolute.
2. God alone receives unqualified obedience without measure; any person lower than God can only receive qualified obedience.
3. Should the delegated authority issue an order clearly contradicting God's command, he will be given submission

but not obedience. We should submit to the person who has received delegated authority from God, but we should disobey the order that offends God.[3]

That leaves us wondering about what responses are appropriate for God's people to take when governing authorities trample justice under foot and themselves come out from under God's authority. We will take up these concerns momentarily, but first we must stop just long enough to consider the fourth principle put to us in Romans 13: God uses the existing governing authorities as tools to achieve our good and his greatest glory. Remember God's words: 'For he [specifically for Paul, Nero and the Roman Empire he led in New Testament days] is God's servant to do you good' (Rom. 13:4)!

Once again, we ask 'Always?' Does God always use the existing governing authorities, no matter how depraved, to bring about our highest good and his greatest glory? The answer is a resolute 'Yes!' Yet with our minds filled with the vivid images of Nero's reign of terror, we wonder, 'How can that be good?' Indeed, we can fill our minds with scenes of the horrors and atrocities perpetrated by numerous dictators throughout the centuries and wonder aloud 'How can that achieve the good of God's people or the glory of our Lord?'

The best answer is found approximately five pages to the left in your Bible. God has already established the principle for the believer which may not answer all our questions, but convinces our will to trust him even under less than ideal governmental leadership. God said, 'And we know that in all things God works for the good of those who love him, who have been called according to his purpose' (Rom. 8:28).

The greater question we must answer is not only, 'Does God always use the existing governing authorities for my good and his glory?' but, 'Am I committed to God's purpose in my life?' That purpose is further described for us, 'For those God foreknew he also predestined to be conformed to the likeness of his Son, that he might be the firstborn among many brothers'

(Rom. 8:29). If you are as committed as God is to the achievement of Christlikeness in your life, God can use anything, yes, even a rotten civil authority, to accomplish it. God has declared that he is able to make even the wrath of man praise him (Ps. 76:10). God can take the most disobedient, debauched, immoral, drunken, perverse leader that the world has ever seen and he can accomplish his purposes through him: 'The king's heart is in the hand of the LORD; he directs it like a watercourse wherever he pleases' (Prov. 21:1).

God is more concerned about our character being conformed to the image of Christ than he is which tool he may use to bring that transformation about. I believe, however, God has a preference about the tools he uses in our sanctification. He prefers to use his Word (John 15:1-2, see our previous chapter also), applying his sword to our lives in order to prune from us those things that keep us from being more fruitful. That is a painful, daily process of personal discipleship – a process only the truly regenerate will prevail in. Yet God will use it to achieve the transformation of our character into that of his Son. God prefers that we willingly come under his authority and that of his Word, and that we allow him to remove from us the things that hinder the expression of his Son in and through us.

If we will not submit to that sanctifying work of God and we choose rather to come out from under the authority of his Word, he will muster others of his delegated authorities and focus them upon our lives to accomplish his great goal of creating Christlikeness in us. I wonder if this does not say, that if indeed the West is headed in the direction many Christians believe it to be headed today, that it is not so much an indictment upon some wicked rulers, but upon the people who name the Name of Jesus Christ and yet refuse to personally come under the authority of God's Word? Then, frustrated and angry at the disobedience of others who in their unregenerate state know no better, the believers rise up and in Jesus' name do carnal things themselves to try to change the

71

country's direction. Is it unthinkable to believe that God would do as he has done previously in history? That God would raise up ungodly rulers to chasten his rebellious people? The answer is not to rebel against the hand of God, but to submit to God and his governing authorities. The answer is found in confession, repentance and mourning over our sin that God might again restore us.

Charles Stanley has given us a word we must hear: 'You never go wrong obeying God. God always conquers. There is tremendous, awesome power in submission.'[4] To illustrate his point, Stanley made a remarkable observation. In Romans 13 you have Paul and Nero. Where is the Rome of Nero today? Where is the Rome of the man who cast Christians to the lions and burned their bodies as torches in his gardens? Where is Nero's Rome? It is no more. A city remains, but it is not the city or the empire of Nero's day. Where, on the other hand, is the church of Jesus Christ? Where is that church which, under the Spirit-inspired guidance of Paul and Peter, learned to submit to the governing authorities even at the cost of their very own lives? The church is being built! The church is advancing! The church is triumphing and the very gates of hell are not prevailing against it! Let us never forget that there is incredible power in submission.

So we have been given several basic principles for how we are to relate to those in governing authority over us. Those principles, as basic and easily stated as they are, raise some bewildering, but answerable questions. As we draw this chapter to a close we would do well to consider biblical responses that Christians can make to those in political office and to whom God has handed a measure of his authority.

Our first response must be to *pray*. 'I urge, then, first of all, that requests, prayers, intercession and thanksgiving be made for everyone – for kings and all those in authority, that we may live peaceful and quiet lives in all godliness and holiness. This is good, and pleases God our Savior' (1 Tim. 2:1-3). We often tip our hat at prayer, but then proceed on our way without having truly sought God. We must remember that, if we have not seriously prevailed in prayer on a consistent basis for our nation and its leaders, we have no basis for complaint against them. Personally, I can say that the majority of the people with whom I am acquainted who complain the loudest and longest about our nation, the government and our elected officials have never once darkened the door of a corporate prayer meeting in our church. We could use a history lesson on how prayer has affected the course of our nation. Absorb the heart-cry of Abraham Lincoln who uttered these words in his Proclamation for a National Day of Fasting, Humiliation and Prayer on April 30, 1863.

> We have been the recipients of the choicest bounties of heaven. We have been preserved these many years in peace and prosperity. We have grown in numbers, wealth and power, as no other nation has ever grown. But we have forgotten God. We have forgotten the gracious hand which preserved us in peace and multiplied and enriched and strengthened us; and we have vainly imagined, in the deceitfulness of our hearts, that all these blessings were produced by some superior wisdom and virtue of our own. Intoxicated with unbroken success, we have become too self-sufficient to feel the necessity of redeeming and preserving grace, too proud to pray to the God that made us! It behooves us, then to humble ourselves before the offended Power, to confess our national sins, and to pray for clemency and forgiveness.[5]

Prayer must be the first work of those who understand and have gladly come under the direct authority of God through his Son Jesus Christ. We may approach the ruling King of the universe and call on him to achieve his glory in and through our nation and its rulers.

Hand in hand with our praying we must *participate* in the process of government. In the Western world we are privileged beyond description to live where we are guaranteed a valid part in the governing process. We must participate through the casting of intelligent and prayerful votes when the opportunity is given to us. As obvious as that may appear, we are told, for example, that only 50% of Christians in America are registered to vote and only 50% of them ever actually do.[6] That is a travesty and grieves the God who gave us the privilege and responsibility of placing people in elected office. We must not only vote, we must participate in the governing process by communicating with those elected to represent us. Again, we learn that less than 20% of people have ever contacted their representatives in any way.[7]

Throughout our involvement by prayer and participation in the process of government we must produce and project a submissive attitude. Unfortunately, conservative, Bible-believing Christians have become known among many in the political arena as hateful and vicious. We who exist because of the love of God ought to lead with love. Instead we are known far too often for what we stand against, rather than what we stand for. Remember, submission has to do with our attitude, obedience has to do with our conduct. We are obligated to render submission to those to whom God has delegated his authority, even if, in extreme circumstances, we cannot render obedience to them. Even if we must disobey, we must still maintain an attitude of submission. We must respect an office, even if we may not be able to respect the person who may be holding that office at any given time.

We must also patiently endure suffering. We must trust God. Yes, it is that simple. We must accept his chastening. We must learn his lessons. 'In repentance and rest is your salvation, *but you would have none of it*' (Isa. 30:15, emphasis mine).

Finally, we must *passionately share* the gospel of Jesus Christ. Somewhere we have picked up the erroneous notion that our mission as the people of Jesus Christ is to reform society. In his caustic but effective way J. Vernon McGee said that we are called of God to catch fish, not to clean out the fish bowl. He further reiterated: 'Christianity is not a movement to improve government or to help society clean up the town. It is to preach the gospel that is the power of God unto salvation which will bring into existence individuals like the men who signed the Declaration of Independence and gave us a government of laws.'[8]

Dr. David L. Rambo, then President of The Christian and Missionary Alliance, spoke with keen analysis of our problem:

> The sad and perilous development of the 1992 campaign is that Christians entered the political arena to push on secular society some issues that are not the core of the gospel we are charged to proclaim.
>
> As a result, millions of Americans may now see evangelicals as bearers of a gospel that is not good news about Jesus Christ, but bad news for abortionists and gays. By our activism, often poorly conceived and stridently promoted, we have created an image of rigid, prejudiced people with whom non-Christians will not want to associate.
>
> More and more Americans will feel entirely justified and respectable saying no to the church. They may not be rejecting Jesus, just the people who profess to follow him. A sign hung prominently in the Clinton campaign headquarters as a reminder for all to see: 'It's the Economy, Stupid.' They identified a principle issue and stuck to it. Evangelicals may do well to post a similar reminder: 'It's the Gospel.' That is what we have been called to proclaim.... Evangelicals must get back to making the main thing the main thing: raising up Jesus Christ as the Son of God and Savior of sinners.[9]

May the God who is able to use the most rebellious ruler to achieve his glory find in us, his people, a more willing party to the promotion of his praise. To him belongs the sovereign right to choose the means by which he does so.

NOTES

1. Merrill C. Tenney, *New Testament Times* (Grand Rapids: William B. Eerdmans Publishing Company, 1965), pp.283-292.

2. See Norman L. Geisler, *Christian Ethics* (Grand Rapids: Baker Book House, 1989), pp. 243-246.

3. Watchman Nee, *Spiritual Authority* (New York: Christian Fellowship Publishers, Inc., 1972), pp.107-109.

4. Charles Stanley, 'A Call To Civil Responsibility' (Atlanta: In Touch Ministries, 1988).

5. W. David Stedman, *Our Ageless Constitution*, (Asheboro, NC: The Steadman Liberty Library, 1987), p. 162.

6. Stanley, Ibid.

7. Ibid.

8. J. Vernon McGee, *Thru The Bible with J. Vernon McGee*, v.4 (Nashville: Thomas Nelson, Inc., 1983), p.736.

9. David L. Rambo, 'Briefing' (Colorado Springs: The Christian and Missionary Alliance, December 1992).

5

The Authority of God and the Church

It was one of those early May mornings that we in the north dream of – winter behind us and spring bursting all around. After a long hard winter the snow was gone and the earth was beginning to warm. I was in my study with my Bible open before me; I was entertaining what I suppose many would describe as pastoral contemplations. Those thoughts were driven away by the sound of the telephone. Pressing the receiver to my ear I answered as I always do, stating the name of our church clearly. There was a prolonged pause on the other end, followed by a few mumbling sounds, as if I had stumped the person on the other end. Finally a woman ventured to ask, 'Do you sell tomato plants?' The church is often asked to be everything to everyone, but never have we even entertained the notion of starting a nursery on the side. I responded, 'We are a church. No, we don't sell tomato plants.' Following a few more mumbles, I heard a click.

People expect a lot from the church; people turn to the church when in need. Often leaders in the church feel wholly inadequate to address those needs. But tomato plants? I am certain my friend on the phone simply dialed the wrong number. Yet tomato plants are not that far removed from some of the requests we in the church receive when people have a need they want us to do something about. 'You're a church, aren't you? Aren't you suppose to help people?,' some spitefully say with an incredulous voice. 'You are supposed to be there when I need you, but otherwise don't get too nosey and intrusive. Keep your distance, but be there for me when I call on you,' is the sentiment of many a modern church shopper. Little wonder that the mention of the words 'authority' and 'church' in the same sentence can grow a church from 200 to twenty in short order.

This is, of course, merely symptomatic of the entire revolt against authority that we have been tracing. John Woodbridge accurately portrays the picture with regard to the church and its message.

> A 'Gospel of Self-fulfillment' swept through the United States in the 1970s and helped nurture the spirit of a perverse narcissism. Anne David, professor of sociology ... puts the matter bluntly: 'Our culture promotes a type of pathological (disturbed) narcissism.... We have a lot of grown-up two year olds out there expecting to be happy now.' Millions of Americans heed the siren-like message of the 'Gospel of Self-Fulfillment.' Now they sense that obeying the Bible's teachings would rain on their narcissistic parade.[1]

Sensing the loss of authority because of the advances of the spirit-of-the-age, the church has relentlessly pursued making its methods and message contemporary. Bowing to the world's techniques have only served to further undermine her authority.

> By responding to market pressures, the church forfeits its authority to proclaim truth and loses its ability to call its members to account. In other words, it can no longer disciple and discipline. But as alien and archaic as the idea may seem, the task of the church is not to make men and women happy; it is to make them holy.[2]

In a world of self-fulfillment there would appear to be no place left for the church, its members, ministries and leaders, unless of course that church is devoid of any standards and will simply pour its resources into whatever 'need' an individual's whim may deem important. Small wonder that the church in North America and Europe is struggling to have a voice in the popular culture. It is estimated that in Europe and North America, an average of 53,000 people leave the Christian church in the span of an average week.[3] At the same time Americans by the millions turn to television talk shows for entertainment, counsel and input on the life issues confronting them. Donahue, Oprah, Sally Jesse, and the like are estimated to have between 2.5 million and 8.6 million viewers each, per day![4] Our flight from absolute truth on the ship of relativism has thrown us into a storm of pragmatism. But the prophets of the pragmatic are always kept at a distance. They dance across the tube, they are encountered while surfing the net or browsing the web, or perhaps we receive their counsel through the written word or via audio or video tape. Regardless of the medium, we have retreated into a privatized world which allows no one personal and direct access to our lives. No one is allowed to come alongside, to challenge us about areas of our life we do not wish them to see. In our revolt against authority we have isolated ourselves and are drowning in our loneliness and subjectivity.

The church is a place of 'one anothers'. We are to honor one another, bear one another's burdens, love one another, exhort one another, and provoke one another, among other things. Such intimacy and vulnerability is too intimidating to many children of the culture. So when church, accountability, authority, leadership, polity, membership, commitment and other such 'scary' words are introduced into conversation people respond by mention of names like Jones, Koresh, Swaggert, Bakker, and Moon. The mere mention of these names is expected to be proof enough that such conversation about this church/authority nonsense need go no further; as if the mention of a few false teachers, heretics, swindlers and adulterers forever buried the church and its leaders.

The notion that the church is vested with authority is a hard sell today. Our concern, however, is not with what is palatable, but with what is true. There is another group, however, that also struggles with authority and the church, albeit for different reasons. Some who are overrun by the pace of life, confused by the plethora of choices, and frightened by the speed of change seem to run to the church with hands frantically clasped over their ears or eyes. Like a child fleeing to their father's lap during a lightening storm, they beg their leaders to 'make it all go away'. 'A horrible and shocking thing has happened in the land: The prophets prophesy lies, and the priests rule by their own authority, *and my people love it this way*' (Jer. 5:30-31, emphasis mine). As self-destructive as an aversion to authority is to the majority of the culture, the blind trust of a smaller segment is equally dangerous.

Does the church have authority? If so, what is that authority like? Authority over what? Or whom? Where do I meet that authority in the church? How is a local church and its members to function with regard to this authority? The questions are legion.

Jesus Christ, being God, has absolute authority (Matt. 28:18). Jesus delegated something of his authority to his apostles who laid the foundation for the church (Eph. 2:20). The apostolic authority has been passed on to us in the canon of New Testament Scripture (2 Tim. 3:16-17; 2 Pet. 3:15-16). The church has been charged to live under the authority of these Scriptures by the power of the Holy Spirit. Those who are vested with leadership wield authority to hold the church to the will of God as expressed in these Scriptures. 'These, then, are the things you should teach. Encourage and rebuke with all authority. Do not let anyone despise you' (Tit. 2:15). There is, then, the authority of God delegated to the church – authority vested in the church collective as it pursues its God-given commission (Matt. 28:18-20), in individual believers as they fulfill their God-ordained place in that commission (Luke 10:17-20; Eph. 1:15-2:7), and in the God-given leaders of the church who are charged to lead the people of God in the fulfilment of their commission and in care for them in the process (Heb. 13:17; 1 Tim. 5:17). We will examine the authority of the church as a whole as it pursues the fulfilment of the Great Commission in chapter ten and the authority of the individual believer in chapter eight. Let us confine ourselves here to the discussion of the authority of leadership in the church. Our questions will be five in number: Do church leaders have legitimate authority in leading the people of God? To what kind of people does God delegate this authority? What do they have authority to do? How do elders gain this leadership authority? Why should I, as a believer in Jesus Christ living at the dawn of the twenty-first century, come under the authority of local church leaders?

Let's first address the question of whether there is legitimate authority delegated by God to individuals so they can lead the church of God. The answer is, yes. As the organization of the New Testament developed more completely we find more instruction given by the writers of Scripture as to its form. 'Let the elders who rule well be considered worthy of double honor, especially those who work hard at preaching and teaching' (1 Tim. 5:17, NASB). The Greek verb translated 'rule' is *proistemi*. The New International Version has rendered it with the unfortunate translation 'direct the affairs of '. The Greek verb clearly carries the idea of authoritative leadership, as seen from a survey of the relevant lexicons and Greek authorities.[5]

Similarly we read in 1 Thessalonians 5:12, 'Now we ask you, brothers, to respect those who work hard among you, *who are over you in the Lord* and who admonish you' (emphasis mine). The Greek participle translated 'are over' is again our word *proistemi*. The word was used in other Greek writings of the day to describe a variety of officials, superintendents, village heads or chiefs, landlords, estate managers and guardians of children.[6] There is legitimate, God-ordained authority vested in those who lead the local church. We must notice, however, as a brief aside, until we can take up this concern more fully in a moment, that such authority is 'in the Lord'. Only God's authority is absolute; all delegated authority is measured and relative, confined to the strictures of God's Word, ways and will. Nevertheless, 'Obey your leaders and submit to their authority', is God's Word to believers today as much as in the first century (Heb. 13:17).

The church is the community of those redeemed by God through Jesus Christ and bound together by the Holy Spirit. Wherever people relate to one another and try to accomplish anything together there must be authority and submission, leaders and followers.

> Life without authority is unthinkable and would be unlivable. Life is surrounded by authority; we live in a context of authority. No kind of association is possible without authority.... The whole business of living together in any way would be impossible without the existence and the acceptance of authority.[7]

The New Testament recognizes this central fact and its writers, under the inspiration of the Holy Spirit, handed us enduring instructions for how the authority of God in the church is to function.

That brings us to our second question, To what kind of people does God delegate this authority? The New Testament yields much about the character of those to whom God would delegate his authority to lead in the church. We have put before us to this point three passages of Scripture which tell us five qualities of those who minister with authority in the leadership of the church.

First, we note that they are *elders*. While the word originally meant a man of advanced years, it came to signify one who exhibited the maturity of Christian character. This is clear from the biblical standards advanced by the apostle Paul for elders. An elder who is worthy of the role passes four tests: the test of a genuine and deep relationship with God, the test of authentic and godly relationships with others, the test of self-control and right perspective on self, and the test of a right relationship to his family.[8] An elder must have a right relationship to God. They must hold firmly to the truths of

Scripture (Tit. 1:9), be upright and holy (Tit. 1:8), able to communicate God's Word (1 Tim. 3:2; 5:17; Tit. 1:9), be above reproach (1 Tim. 3:2; Tit. 1:6), be established in their relationship with God (1 Tim. 3:6), be zealous after what is good (Tit. 1:8). They must also pass the test of right relationships with others. They must be respectable (1 Tim. 3:2), hospitable (1 Tim. 3:2; Tit. 1:8), not argumentative (1 Tim. 3:3), not violent, but gentle (1 Tim. 3:3; Tit. 1:7), be well respected by those outside the church (1 Tim. 3:7), not overbearing (Tit. 1:7), and not zealous after dishonest gain (Tit. 1:7). Likewise, the elder who will exercise authority in the local church must pass the test of rightly relating to himself. He must be disciplined (Tit. 1:8), temperate (Tit. 1:7), not held by a desire for money (1 Tim. 3:3), self-controlled (1 Tim. 3:2; Tit. 1:8), able to control his temper (Tit. 1:7), and not given to drunkenness (1 Tim. 3:3; Tit. 1:7). Finally, the elder must rightly relate to his family members. He must have one wife (1 Tim. 3:2), have obedient children (1 Tim. 3:4-5; Tit. 1:6), and manage his family well (1 Tim. 3:4; Tit. 1:6).

The second thing we note about those to whom God delegates his authority to lead in the local church is that they must be *hard workers*. The elders who are to be honored by the people they lead are they 'who work hard at preaching and teaching' (1 Tim. 5:17). God does not delegate his authority to the lazy or self-serving. There is no delegated authority for the shepherd who feeds himself from of the sheep.

> This is what the Sovereign LORD says: Woe to the shepherds of Israel who only take care of themselves! Should not shepherds take care of the flock? You eat the curds, clothe yourselves with the wool and slaughter the choice animals, but you do not take care of the flock. You have not strengthened the weak or healed the sick or bound up the injured. You have not brought back the strays or searched for the lost. You have ruled them harshly and brutally ... therefore, O shepherds, hear the word of the LORD: This is what the Sovereign LORD says: I am against the shepherds and will hold them accountable for my flock. I will remove them from

tending the flock so that the shepherds can no longer feed themselves (Ezek. 34:2-5, 9-10).

As noted earlier, the one to whom God delegates his authority does so 'in the Lord' (1 Thess. 5:12). The authority of church leaders is not arbitrary and unilateral, but bounded within the sphere of the activities assigned by the Lord through the Word of God. This marks off the authority of elders as distinctly different from all other delegated authorities and limited to the confines of God's instructions to them.

> The added phrase 'in the Lord' defines the nature and scope of their leadership. They are not secular leaders dealing with civic or political affairs but rather preside in connection with the spiritual concerns of the saints. Their position does not stem from personal ambition but rather from their spiritual maturity. Their position of leadership in the church is based upon the recognized fact that they and those being led are 'in the Lord'. 'His Lordship underlies their leadership.' Their authority is not that of a formal ecclesiastical hierarchy but rather is 'one exercised in the warmth of Christian bonds.'[9]

Their authority being 'in the Lord' means that they know what it is to personally live under authority. In fact the delegated authority who pleases God always seeks to live under authority – God's and the authority of those to whom God has called them to submit. The biblical model is for a plurality of leadership within the local church (Acts 14:23; 20:17; Phil. 1:1; Tit. 1:5). Neither does the authority and function of elders extend beyond the local church in which they serve.[10] This means that the individual elder did not wield authority independently, but only as one of a body of elders. Each individual elder is to be in submission to the whole of the elders. Elders are not above examination, and indeed are to be held responsible for failure to live up to the standards outlined by Scripture (1 Tim. 5:19-22). True delegated authority looks for its God-given authorities and delights to submit to them.

The kind of person to whom God delegates his authority for ministry in the church is also indicated by their being called *leaders* (Heb. 13:17). The Greek noun translated here is *hegeomai* and is used elsewhere to describe military leaders, national leaders, princes, and leading priests.[11] Jesus, however, also used the word and forever transformed the kind of person who is fit to serve as one of his 'leaders'.

> Also a dispute arose among them as to which of them was considered to be greatest. Jesus said to them, 'The kings of the Gentiles lord it over them; and those who exercise authority over them call themselves Benefactors. But you are not to be like that. Instead, the greatest among you should be like the youngest, and the one who rules like the one who serves' (Luke 22:24-26).

Indeed, Jesus personally transformed what it means to be a leader among his people: 'I am among you as one who serves' (v.27). Those worthy of exercising God's delegated authority in the church know the difference between the authority of God-ordained service to the saints and the selfishness of authoritarianism.

> Exercise of authority in its various spheres is not necessarily authoritarian. There is a crucial distinction here. Authoritarianism is authority corrupted, gone to seed. Authoritarianism appears when the submission that is demanded cannot be justified in terms of truth or morality. Nazism, Communism and Jim Jones' cult in Guyana are examples. Any form of human authority can degenerate in this way. You have authoritarianism in the state when the regime uses power in an unprincipled way to maintain itself. You have it in churches when leaders claim control of their followers' consciences. You have it in academic work at high school, university or seminary when you are required to agree with your professor rather than follow the evidence of truth for yourself. You have it in the family when parents direct or restrict their children unreasonably. Unhappy experiences of authority are usually experiences of degenerate authority, that is, of authoritarianism. That such experiences leave a bad taste and proper skeptisim about authority in all its forms is sad but not surprising.[12]

Finally God delegates his authority in the local church to those *who are focused on the Word of God*. These are the ones who labor hard in 'preaching and teaching' (1 Tim. 5:17). Elders who are vested with God's authority are those who focus the people they lead on the Scriptures, not on themselves or on secondary issues. To do this they must focus themselves on and submit themselves to the Word of God. '... true elders do not dictate, but direct. They do not command the consciences of their brethren, but appeal to their brethren to faithfully follow God's Word.'[13]

To what kind of person does God delegate his authority to lead the church? To men whose character and relationships qualify them to be an elder in the New Testament sense of that word, to men whose hearts have been so captivated with the Lord Jesus that their lives are compelled in the hard work of service to his saints, to men who understand what it is to be 'in the Lord' and who focus their ministry on that sphere, to men who lead by serving, and to men who ever focus their lives, and the lives of those they lead, upon the Word of God. To these kind of men, and only to these kind of men, does God delegate his authority to lead in the local church.

> Out of love they suffer and bear the brunt of difficult people and problems so the lambs are not bruised. They bear the misunderstanding and sins of others so the assembly may live in peace. They lose sleep so others may rest. They make great personal sacrifices of time and energy for the welfare of others. They see themselves as men under authority. They depend on God for wisdom and help, not on their own power and cleverness. They face the false teachers' fierce attacks. They guard the community's liberty and freedom in Christ so the saints are encouraged to develop their gifts, mature, and serve one another.[14]

We have seen the kind of man God chooses to delegate his authority to in the local church, but what exactly do they have authority to do? Since the slide from servant-leadership to authoritarianism is greased with the fat of human pride, we must define ourselves carefully. The New Testament seems to identify three broad areas of leadership the elders of the local church are to take. These are the God-given arenas in which he has designed his authority, delegated to the elders, to operate in. They are not mutually exclusive from one another and overlap is apparent. Yet distinguishing them enables us to identify more carefully the areas of authority for local church elders.

The first area of authority is that of *leadership*. The elder is called an 'overseer' (Tit. 1:7; 1 Pet. 5:2). The Greek term translated here (*episkopos*) comes from the Greek political realm and in secular usages designated a presiding official of a civic organization. An overseer is one who is placed in a position where they can and are responsible to 'see over' the body of people they are to lead. From that higher vantage point of leadership they are responsible to watch out for the needs of people that may go unnoticed by those who make up that body (Acts 20:28), and to direct the body in ministering to those needs. Likewise, from the perspective of leadership they are responsible to look forward to where the church should be and is indeed headed in ministry (1 Tim. 3:5; 5:17), and help stimulate them toward the fulfillment of their God-given commission. They are to scan the body of people they lead and make certain that it is truth and not error that they are feeding on (Acts 20:28-31). In this oversight of the body they use always as their measuring rod the Word of God (1 Tim. 3:2; 5:17). The elders' leadership authority never extends beyond the written Word of God. Elders have authority to take the lead in the congregation, it is ever servant-leadership, but it is and must be truly leadership.

The elders are also given *authority to shepherd* the people given to their charge (Acts 20:28; 1 Pet. 5:2). The image of a shepherd is one that carried strong Old Testament overtones and whose responsibilities and powers were shaped by men like David and the Old Testament prophets (Ps. 23; Is. 40:11;

Jer. 31:10; Ezek. 34:5, 12). Elders are under-shepherds in that the church is God's flock (Acts 20:28), Jesus is the Chief Shepherd (1 Pet. 5:4), and he is the great Shepherd of the sheep (Heb. 13:20). The standard for their work is Jesus himself who is the Good Shepherd (John 10:11). As shepherds, then, they feed the sheep (Tit. 1:9), protect them from harm (Acts 20:2-31), heal their wounds (Jas. 5:14), and, by going before their sheep, lead by example (1 Pet. 5:3). All of this gives the strong implication that elder-shepherds must be close to their people. They spend time with them, talk with them, pursue them, work with them, play with them, laugh with them, cry with them and in every way possible share life with them. Shepherding cannot be done from a boardroom. Elders are overseers, but that must never be understood as divorced from their role as day-by-day care-givers to the people.

One painful part of getting close enough to people to shepherd them is that you are close enough to see their dirt. That means elders must do the work of correcting and admonishing the people God has set them apart to shepherd and lead (Tit. 1:10-16). The most painful part of leadership is the necessity of leading the way when church discipline is needed. Discipline is something the entire body is responsible for, but often the elders will lead the way.

Few issues could be more politically incorrect than the notion of church discipline. The courts have a field day with lawsuits brought against churches by former members who have been disciplined.[15] Yet the church has the authority given by her Lord to discipline his people in certain instances (Matt. 18:15-20; Tit. 3:10-11; 2 Thess. 3:14-15; Gal. 6:1-5).

> ... no one should expect to join a church (which, after all, involves a free decision) and then refuse to accept its authority (its rules, if you will). For failing to attend a few meetings, one can be thrown out of the Rotary Club. For failing to live up to a particular dress code, one can be dismissed from most private clubs. For failing to perform the required community service, one can be thrown out of the Junior League.

Yet when the church imposes discipline – denying the benefits of membership to those who flout its standards – it is charged with everything short of (and sometimes including) fascism.

But shouldn't the church have at least the same right to set its standards as the Rotary Club? People who don't like it can and should go elsewhere. We weaken the church when we fail to discipline.[16]

Despite the painful nature of the work, elders who honor God and love the people given to their care by him will lead the way in discipline. There must be much self-examination in the process, realizing that they too are subject to the same process (1 Tim. 5:19-20). There must be much prayer and patience exhibited. There must be humility and tears. But there must also be follow-through if needed.

This leads us to the third broad area of ministry that the elders have authority to lead in – they are to serve as *representatives of the whole church* in certain circumstances. When Paul wanted to touch the Ephesian church as he passed on his way to Jerusalem, it was the elders that he called for and met with (Acts 20:17). Elders were listed along with the apostles when Paul came to find an answer to a doctrinal dispute (Acts 15:2, 4, 6, 22). Likewise the elders were chosen to represent the church by responsible handling of the relief funds sent to Jerusalem (Acts 11:29-30). It is clear that to represent the church, elders must know the desires, positions, goals, and determinations of the people. Only servant-leaders will serve well in this regard.

This leads us to our fourth question, how do elders come by this leadership authority? The apostle Paul made plain that the position, ministry and authority of elders are not gained by their choice, nor even by the choice of the people they lead. The only one who can make a man an elder is God. 'Keep watch over yourselves and all the flock of which the Holy Spirit has made you overseers' (Acts 20:28).

> Spiritual leaders are not made by election or appointment, by men or any combination of men, or by conferences or synods. Only God can make them. Simply holding a position of importance does not constitute one a leader. Nor does taking courses in leadership or resolving to become a leader.... Spiritual leadership is a thing of the Spirit and is conferred by God alone. When his searching eye alights on a man who has qualified, he anoints him with his Spirit and separates him to his distinctive ministry (Acts 9:17; 22:21).[17]

The New Testament records elders being appointed by the apostles or their designates (Acts 14:23; Tit. 1:5). But in practical terms, how should men become elders today? That direct line of apostolic authority has been broken with the passing of the apostles (in the limited sense of the word), yet their authority is bound up for us in the New Testament writings which the Spirit guided them in writing. It would seem that the appropriate pattern for selection of elders today would be for the church to identify those men who are willing and desirous (1 Tim. 3:1) of the ministry of eldership and then examine their lives according to the qualifications given us in Scripture (1 Tim. 3:1ff; Tit. 1:6ff). Depending upon a church's polity, the actual selection may be made by the whole congregation (via a vote at a business meeting) or through some body delegated with responsibility and authority to select elders for them (perhaps by those already serving as elders). The key is that those men whom God has selected be identified and that the people place these men forward so as to recognize God's selection.

Perhaps the image we need to put before our minds once again is that of David and the road he traveled to the palace in Jerusalem. In chapter two we saw David's patient refusal to lay hold of authority before God's time. He did not exercise the authority of kingship until both God and the people had anointed him as king. During those approximately fourteen years of waiting between the time God anointed him as king and the time the people recognized God's anointing and added theirs as well, David waited patiently. A man may desire to be an elder (1 Tim. 3:1), and if he does it is a fine work he desires to do. But a man's desire to serve, even his personal sense that God has chosen him to serve as an elder, does not make the process complete. The people, having studied the man and held his life and ministry up against the Scriptural qualifications of an elder, must, through whatever means their fellowship provides for, recognize God's anointing upon the man and add theirs to it.

Despite a close investigation of the kind of men to whom God delegates authority for leadership in the church and an understanding of the areas in which they have authorization to exercise that authority, some are desperate to ask our final question. Why should I, as one living in this day and age, come under the authority of the leadership of a local church? Authority, biblically understood and exercised, should never be seen as a threat, but rather as a warm place of safety. However, because the notion runs so deeply contrary to our natural bent toward autonomy, we demand good reason to submit ourselves to any authority. Fortunately God graciously bows to feed our apprehension with the soothing reasons of his mind.

Each believer in Jesus Christ should come under the authority of a good local church and the leaders there because it is one of the key ways God guards our lives. 'Obey your leaders and submit to their authority. They keep watch over you' (Heb. 13:17). 'Keep watch' carries the idea of depriving one's self of sleep to serve as an alert sentry, posted over someone or something you care deeply for.[18] The image that the writer desired to draw for our mind's eye is that of a shepherd depriving himself of sleep throughout the long night as he grazed his sheep in a particularly dangerous area. In fact the pronoun 'they' is emphatic, yielding the notion that it is 'they and no one else' who selflessly watch out for your souls.[19] Indeed it is hard to find others in this world whom we can trust to have only our good in mind.

A second reason we should submit to the leadership of our local church is because they are accountable to God for their service and use of his authority. 'They keep watch over you as men who must give an account' (Heb. 13:17). Jesus raised the bar for all who would seek to serve him by serving others, 'From everyone who has been given much, much will be demanded; and from the one who has been entrusted with much, much more will be asked' (Luke 12:48). It is an awesome thought to me that I will one day literally stand before my Lord and be called to give an accounting to him for how I have applied his grace, extended his resources and used his authority in leading and caring for his people. I need every cooperation from his people now to be able to rightly stand before him then.

May I say a word to you who may just now be a bit disappointed by your local church? Beware of becoming overly enamored with the visiting preacher who fills the pulpit during your pastor's vacation, the parachurch ministry that stops in once a year to make a presentation, and the great crusader or teacher you happen to hear one day on the radio or see on television. Do not mistake what I am saying, they are no doubt wonderful servants of God. Do not, however, confuse their wonderful and legitimate ministries with your need for shepherds who will be there tomorrow, when the traveling evangelist has moved on to another city. Value the local leaders who will not only answer your questions, but, when you are struggling to apply their counsel from God's Word, will still be there for you. The advice of the talk-show counselor is fine, but don't forget that you also need someone on site with you who will not put you on hold or hang up when the implications of their advice runs into commercial time. Outside ministries often look very exciting to weary saints; always on top, achieving nothing but victories. But there is often very little accountability – you to them and they to you. Don't underestimate the value of those who day-by-day, week-by-week, year-by-year stand with you.

It is tough to be held in such accountability by the Lord, therefore make their ministry as easy as you can. Your encouragement, service, ready and willing spirit, prayers, and submission make not only their service easier, but also glorify God. God promises elders who serve well 'the crown of glory that will never fade away' (1 Pet. 5:4). That reward is a powerful motivator to serve well. You can assist them in fulfilling the requirement to serve well by your attitudes, motivations and action.

A third reason we are to submit to the leaders of our local church is that it will bring them joy in their service to God. 'Obey them so that their work will be a joy, not a burden' (Heb. 13:17). You want leaders who see their service as a joy. When ministry becomes only a burden to bear, it is difficult to refrain from becoming surly, cynical, narrow-minded, and self-serving. Your submissive followership can make their service a deep delight to them and a better experience for you. That is the very point of the final reason to submit to the leadership of your local church.

We should seek out a good local church and joyfully come under the authority of the leaders there because it is for our own good. 'Obey them so that their work will be a joy, not a burden, for that would be of no advantage to you' (Heb. 13:17).

The author's remark is an intentional understatement. It is a literary device, called a *litotes*, in which a milder, negative statement is used instead of a strong, affirmative statement. It is the opposite of a hyperbole. (For example, instead of saying, 'really great work', we might say, 'not bad work'.) The expression causes the reader to stop, think, and fill in the fuller meaning. Stated positively, this clause would read, 'that is harmful to you', or 'that is disastrous for you'.[20]

The church today is asked to be everything to everyone – a painfully impossible assignment. The church must know her Lord and know his commission, and focus its people and their varied gifts, resources, ideas, wishes, and hopes upon his glory and the completion of his commission. For that to happen God has designed there to be leaders who will lead with his vision, serve with his heart, minister by his Spirit, and shepherd with his authority.

> The overriding need of the church, if it is to discharge its obligation to the rising generation, is for a leadership that is authoritative, spiritual and sacrificial. *Authoritative*, because people love to be led by one who knows where he is going and who inspires confidence. They follow almost without question the man who shows himself wise and strong, who adheres to what he believes. *Spiritual*, because leadership that is unspiritual, that can be explained in terms of the natural, although ever so attractive and competent, will result only in sterility and moral and spiritual bankruptcy. *Sacrificial*, because modeled on the life of the One who gave himself a sacrifice for the whole world, who left us an example that we should follow his steps.[21]

May God grant to his church those who will lead with authority, spirituality, and sacrifice. May he also grant that a train of spirit-filled, submissive saints would fall in behind them as they lead onward in the fulfillment of Christ's Great Commission.

NOTES

1. John D. Woodbridge, 'Recent Interpretations of Biblical Authority Part I: A Neo-orthodox (Historiography under Siege,' *Bibliotheca Sacra* 142, January-March, 1985): 4, 5.

2. Charles W. Colson, *The Body* (Dallas: Word Publishing, 1992), p.46.

3. David Bosch, 'Vision for Mission', *International Review of Mission*, January 1987, p.13.

4. Statistics Nielsen Media Research cited in A. Bunce, 'Shock Talk', *Christian Science Monitor*, 5. October 1988, 7-8 and quoted by Charles Colson in *The Body* (Dallas: Word Publishing, 1992), p.161.

5. W. F. Arndt and F. W. Gingrich, in *A Greek-English Lexicon of the*

New Testament and other Early Christian Literature gives the primary meaning as 'be the head of, rule, direct' (pp.713-714); *A Greek-English Lexicon of the New Testament* by Joseph Henry Thayer determines that in the perfect tense (as 1 Tim. 5:17 is) it means '*to be over, to superintend, preside over*' (pp.539-540, emphasis theirs). Moulton and Milligan in *The Vocabulary of the Greek New Testament* give the meaning as 'put before, set over, and intransitively; preside, rule, govern' (p. 541). Moulton, Geden and Moulton in the *Concordance To The Greek New Testament* find that from the first Christian ecclesiastical use of the word in Acts 11:30 and similar usages (Acts 14:23; 15:2, 4, 6, 22, 23; 16:4; 20:17; 21:18) to 1 Timothy 5:17 the concept of rule, direct and authority is present. Lothar Coenen in *The New International Dictionary of New Testament Theology* lists the meaning as 'be at the head of, rule, be concerned about' (1:192).

6. John Stott, *The Message of 1 and 2 Thessalonians* (Downers Grove, Illinois: Inter-Varsity Press, 1991) p.120.

7. William Barclay, *By What Authority?* (Valley Forge, Pennsylvania: Judson Press, 1974), p.199.

8. H. Wayne House, *Charts of Christian Theology and Doctrine* (Grand Rapids, Michigan: Zondervan Publishing House, 1992), p.119.

9. D. Edmond Hiebert, *1 and 2 Thessalonians* (Chicago: Moody Press, 1992), p.249.

10. Ed Glassock, 'The Biblical Concept of Elder', *Bibliotheca Sacra*, 144, (January-March, 1987), p.75.

11. F. Buchsel, II, 'hegeomai', Geoffrey W. Bromiley, *Theological Dictionary of the New Testament*, Abridged in one volume (Grand Rapids, Michigan: William B. Eerdmans Publishing Company, 1985), p.303.

12. J. I. Packer, *Authority and Freedom* (Oakland: International Council on Biblical Inerrancy, 1981), p.8.

13. Alexander Strauch, *Biblical Eldership* (Littleton, Colorado: Lewis and Roth Publishers, 1988), p.37.

14. Ibid.

15. For one account see Charles Colson, *Kingdoms In Conflict* (New York: Harper and Row Publishers, 1987), pp. 313ff.

16. Colson, *The Body*, p. 127.

17. J. Oswald Sanders, *Spiritual Leadership* (Chicago: Moody Press, 1967), pp.17-18.

18. Fritz Riencecker, *Linguistic Key to the Greek New Testament* (Grand Rapids, Michigan: Zondervan Publishing House, 1980), p.720.

19. Leon Morris, 'Hebrews' in *The Expositors Bible Commentary* (Grand Rapids, Michigan: Zondervan Publishing House, 1981), 12:152.

20. Strauch, pp.164-165.

21. Sanders, pp.16-17.

6

The Authority of God and Marriage

I looked at the young man and woman standing before me and I said, 'You will now share in the exchange of vows.' I led the nervous groom phrase by phrase through the verbalization of his commitments to God and his soon-to-be wife. I then turned to the bride. Under the watchful eye of teary family members and smiling friends, I too smiled and said gently, 'Sandra, now repeat after me. I, Sandra, take you, Paul, to be my wedded husband.' With quiet but hopeful voice she followed my lead, looking deep into the eyes of her beloved, 'I Sandra, take you Paul, to be my wedded husband.' 'To have and to hold, from this day forward,' I said. Once again she repeated, 'To have and to hold, from this day forward.' 'For better, for worse.' 'For better, for worse.' And so we continued in that beautiful, rhythmic personalization of the sacred vows of marriage. 'And to obey, till death parts us,' I continued. Long pause. Nothing. Quietness. Uncomfortable silence. A lump formed in my throat. In that everlasting moment I confess to having had the fleeting thought, 'She doesn't want to say "obey"! What am I going to do? I know we covered this in the premarital counseling! What is the problem?' I lifted my eyes from the notes I held on top of my Bible, preparing myself to carefully study her face and take a reading of the need of the moment. What I saw, however, was a bride whose face was as white as her dress and whose eyes were beginning to roll back in her head. I moved quickly enough to catch her just before she hit the floor.[1]

It was not the notion of promising before God and man to obey her husband that caused this lovely young bride to pass out, it was the sweltering heat of a mid-August evening. A few minutes and a number of cold compresses later she did indeed finish her vows (this time seated on the piano bench I had pulled in from nearby) – including the promise to obey her husband.

Sandra was overcome by the heat, but I can imagine that I would have lost a good number of other brides and grooms simply over the notion of such an authority structure in the home. In the politically correct world in which we live many people at the altar would cry 'blasphemy' over the 'antiquated' notion of the wife promising to come under the authority of the husband.

The debate over authority in the home does not end with the discussion of the roles of husband and wife. Today even the notion of parental authority over children is distasteful to the current cultural palate. For now, however, let's begin by considering the authority of God within the husband/wife relationship, and then return in the next chapter to consider how his authority is practically expressed between the parents and children.

In plain fashion Paul stated: 'Now I want you to realize that the head of every man is Christ, and the head of the woman is man, and the head of Christ is God' (1 Cor. 11:3). What the apostle stated plainly, the church has in recent decades scrambled thoroughly. The first word to consider is 'head', the English translation of the Greek word *kephale*. The meaning of this word was largely undisputed until Stephen Bedale introduced a new notion in his 1954 article in the *Journal of Theological Studies*.[2] Bedale's innovation was the assertion that *kephale* does not carry the notion of 'authoritative leadership' as traditionally understood, but rather that it means 'source' or 'origin'. In the culturally tumultuous decades that have followed the appearance of Bedale's article, many have seized upon his statements and championed an entirely new notion of the structure of the home. However, in the last several years there have arisen several convincing studies which show that the concept of 'authoritative leadership' understood by the church throughout the centuries should not be thrown out with such cavalier abandon.[3] These studies have once again shown that the meaning of *kephale* contains the notion of authority. In fact Wayne Grudem has successfully proven that there is not one example in all of ancient Greek literature of the word *kephale* being used to refer to a person and still carrying the notion of 'non-authoritative source'.[4]

We will leave the detailed lexical battle to those more qualified than I to speak to such matters and whose findings we may read elsewhere. Let's satisfy ourselves here by noticing the presentation of our current passage as God has given it to us. The debate over the passage comes because our modern sensibilities are offended by the phrase 'the head of the woman is man'. The offended cry, 'It cannot mean "authority"! How can a loving God say that the man has authority over the woman? No, no! God does not mean to say "Man is in authority over woman" but rather that "Man is the source or origin out of which woman was originally taken!"'

Notice, however, the corollary order also given: 'the head of Christ is God'. If 'head' here means 'source' or 'origin', as some contend, then how are we to understand this description of the relationship of the First and Second Persons of the Trinity? In what rationally and theologically sound sense can one say that God the Father is the 'source' or 'origin' of God the Son? Indeed, the logical and theological implications of the attack on the one phrase ('the head of the woman is man') has begun to lead to some heretical notions of the understanding of the other phrase ('the head of Christ is God').[5] The historic understanding of the orthodox doctrine of the Trinity has understood the ontological equality of the members of the Trinity (the Father, Son and Holy Spirit are co-equal, co-eternal, and each alike share completely in the very essence of deity), while upholding the differentiation of redemptive roles for each of the members of the Trinity. The church has from its earliest days understood those differentiations to be eternal distinctions, without in the slightest way diminishing the eternal, divine equality of all three members of the Trinity.[6] The gospel message is that the Father sent and the Son went. The Father initiated and the Son responded. The Father initiated our salvation (Eph. 1:3-6), the Son procured our salvation (Eph. 1:7-12), and the Spirit applies that salvation to us personally (Eph. 1:13-14). While the Father, Son and Holy Spirit remain co-eternal, co-equal and equally share in the essence of deity, for the purposes of redemption they willingly took on different roles. In the divine plan of redemption the Second Person of the Trinity willingly placed himself under the headship of the First Person of the Trinity that their eternal good purpose for our lives might be worked out in time and space. Indeed when the redemptive plan is brought to its completion 'the Son himself will be made subject to him who put everything under him, so that God may be all in all' (1 Cor. 15:28). There is, within the Trinity, no subordination of essence as to divinity, but there is a subordination of role for the purpose of mission.

Headship and submission does not imply inferiority, but rather role and responsibility. Does this not lay bare one of the most deceptive lies of our age? The lie is that if I cannot do what you do, I am not as good as you. One can hear the rustle of demons' wings all around that notion. But my personal worth is not determined by what I can do, but by whose I am!

Notice again 1 Corinthians 11:3: 'The head of Christ is God.' Notice then, 'the head of woman is man.' This headship does not imply inferiority or servility. It means that for the outworking of God's good plan in this world he has determined that there should be equality of personhood and worth, while differentiation in role. Men and women are equals – equal in worth, in the home, before God, in nature, personhood, dignity, service, work, character, godliness, competence, giftedness, intelligence, significance and spiritual insight. But men and

100

women are different by design and we do have different God-given roles. God has designed that, following the order of his own nature and saving pattern, the one should function as the authoritative head, leader, provider, and initiator and the other should function as the helper, supporter, responder and companion.

For all of the controversy over the notion of authority of husband over wife, I am convinced that our problem is not with the fact of God-delegated authority within the home. Our problem is with what we assume that authority means for how we will function in the home. Too often people have read such biblical passages and mentally inserted an erroneous concept of authority as they read them. A husband in authority over his wife – it conjures up mental images of a bigoted, ill-tempered, selfish male who places unreasonable demands upon his wife and if she does not comply he has every right to force her compliance. Nothing could be further from the biblical understanding of authority in the husband/wife relationship.

To clarify our misinformed assumptions about authority in marriage, let's examine the passage that undoubtedly comes to most people's minds when they think of the headship of the husband. It never ceases to amaze me how a man who claims he can't memorize Scripture can quote Ephesians 5:22 word for word. Suddenly his rational powers are sharpened, his mind is clear, his eyes sparkle and he quotes, 'Wives, submit to your husbands as to the Lord.' Yet perhaps the ten verses of the Bible most neglected by males are the ones that follow immediately upon the heels of verse 22. It is these ten verses that describe the realm and responsibility of that delegated authority. When one understands the increased accountability God places upon those to whom he delegates his authority, it heightens still more the man's natural aversion to these verses.

Remember delegated authority is not absolute authority. Only God possesses absolute authority. Every creature will meet with and eventually submit to that authority – either in the joyful submission of discipleship to Christ or in the teeth-gritting, fist-clenched compulsion to bow the knee to Christ on the last day (Phil. 2:10). The authority the husband is commissioned to exercise is not unlimited, rather God has bounded it on all sides. Ephesians 5:23-33 outlines the four boundaries within which he has confined his delegated authority to the husband. Within the limitations of these boundaries, the husband has the responsibility to exercise the authority of God in loving leadership of his wife.

The first boundary line God draws for the authority of the husband is the boundary line of *sacrifice*. God grants to the husband the authority to sacrifice himself for the sake of his wife. That may not sound much like authority if you are working off of the world's definition. However, authority and sacrifice complement one another perfectly, if you understand God's definition.

The Bible declares that the authority of a husband is like unto that of Christ's with the church. 'Husbands, love your wives, just as Christ loved the church and gave himself up for her' (Eph. 5:25). How does Christlike authority reveal itself in the home? Authority begins by loving as Christ loved the church, that is by the act of giving up self for another's benefit.

Men, God has given us authority in the home, not so that we can make certain we get our way. Nor even that we make certain our wives get their way. Rather God has delegated his authority to us to make sure that he gets his way in our home. His way is that his authority and leadership be expressed primarily through servant leaders who sacrifice themselves for the welfare of the others in the family, trusting their personal needs to Christ so they can look to the welfare of others.

What does this mean practically? Jesus' supreme expression of sacrifice for the church was on the cross. As a husband, where is your supreme expression of sacrifice for your wife? I believe it will help us identify those places of needed sacrifice if we call to mind the things Jesus said while making his supreme sacrifice for us.

Jesus said, 'Father, forgive them, for they do not know what they are doing' (Luke 23:34). What do you need to forgive your wife for? Have the years buried some unresolved conflict that has festered and come between you? Or is there something from your last conversation this morning as you were on your way out the door that you need to resolve with her? Forgiveness means you release the other from any obligation for the wrong and that you take full responsibility for the consequences of the wrong they have done to you. Are you willing to make certain she does not have to pay for the wrongs she has done you? That is what Jesus did for us. What consequences do you need to relieve your wife of and take responsibility for?

While on the cross Jesus said to a sinful criminal who had not a righteous bone in his body, 'Today you will be with me in paradise' (Luke 23:43). What is your wife unworthy of today? She is no more perfect than you are. Yet she probably deserves more credit than you give her. What can you give to her today that comes out of free grace without any effort on her part to merit it?

Jesus, on the cross and concerned for his mother's well-being, said to her and to the apostle John, 'Dear woman, here is your son' and 'Here is your mother' (John 19:26-27). In what way can you lay aside your own needs that painfully cry out to you for relief and instead focus on providing for or protecting your wife in some way that will satisfy a timely need in her life?

Jesus also questioned, 'My God, my God, why have you forsaken me?' (Matt. 27:46). With these words our Savior revealed to us that sacrificial love has a price. Where in your life are the lonely places? Marriage was given to us because God looked upon man and said it is not good that he be alone. But with the introduction of sin into the race we began to alienate ourselves from one another and turn inward in self-protection rather than giving lovingly and vulnerably to one another. The loneliness of marriage is a fact. If you truly live life selflessly toward your spouse you will be ushered into moments of profound loneliness, but in those moments you will meet your Savior more intimately than ever possible if you look out only for yourself. You need to willingly face your loneliness and draw near to your Savior entrusting your needs to him rather than manipulating your wife to meet them.

Jesus cried out, 'I am thirsty' (John 19:28) and in so doing revealed his complete humanness and vulnerability. Where, in your relationship with your wife, does your humanness most show itself?

Jesus in victory declared, 'It is finished' (John 19:30)! Jesus was letting the world know that all that would ever be necessary for our salvation was procured for us in his death for us. You are not the Savior, but you are called to exercise his authority by sacrificing yourself for your wife. In what way can you address one of your wife's needs by serving her with a spirit that says, 'Here! It is finished! You need add nothing more'?

Jesus, with his last physical breath, cried out, 'Father, into your hands I commit my spirit' (Luke 23:46). Men, in all frankness, this is the bottom line of our authority. We must fully commit ourselves to God and in service to our wives without expecting or demanding anything from her. You may receive many benefits from her in return for your sacrificial love and leadership or you may never receive the reciprocating love you dream of, but either way you must shut yourself up to God alone as the provider for your every need.

God gives the husband authority in the home – authority to sacrifice himself for his wife. Elizabeth Elliot has written these searching words concerning the role of the husband.

Ponder this love ... It's a far cry from the soupy, selfish sentiment the world calls love. It's got nothing to do with it, really. It's a high and holy summons to forget yourself. 'Forget myself? No way.' That's a normal human response. There is no way, of course, except by the grace of God. We're called to participate with Christ in his own work, to love with his love, to do what he does to and for one another. There's no way in the world to do it alone. We do it because he lives his life in us. When you find yourself saying, 'But isn't it about time I got a little appreciation; doesn't she have any responsibility? Hey, I'm doing it all!' its time to review the standard, 'the same sort of love Christ gave'. You want your wife to submit? Then take a long, steady look at the sort of love Christ gave. It was based on self-sacrifice. That is the basis for authority. It starts with sacrifice. It is maintained by sacrifice.[7]

Tough to swallow? Satan has a counterfeit for all of God's good gifts. He whispers, 'Sacrifice her for your good, use her to meet your needs! Do it under the banner of "headship" or "leadership". Try to make her think it is all for her good and by God's design.' God, however, has delegated his authority to you so that you might sacrifice yourself for her, just as his Son gave himself for you.

God sets another boundary on his authority delegated to the husband. The purpose of Christ sacrificing himself for the church was 'to make her holy, cleansing her by the washing with water through the word, and to present her to himself as a radiant church, without stain or wrinkle or any other blemish, but holy and blameless' (Eph. 5:26-27). This, then, in parallel fashion becomes the reason for a husband to sacrifice his own interests for the welfare of his wife. The second boundary line that marks out the legitimate use of a husband's God-given authority is that of *sanctification*. Self-sacrifice for the purpose of setting your wife apart in a special way that only she can fulfil.

What does it mean to sanctify something? It means to set something apart from an ordinary purpose to a special one. Illustrations of sanctification are all around us. Your wife may say to you, 'Don't cut sandpaper with those sizzors! They are my good ones.' She has a pair reserved for special uses and a pair for ordinary tasks. Or you may say to your son when he arrives home from school, 'Go to your room and change out of your school clothes before you go out to play.' He has some clothes for everyday use and others for special occasions.

The boundary of authority known as sanctification arises from the loving ministry of Jesus to his church. How does he sanctify his people? He uses the Word of God (v.26). Jesus told his disciples, 'You are already clean because of the word I have spoken to you' (John 15:3). Through this washing with the Word of God Jesus set his people apart. Apart to whom? himself! How? In all her glory and full potential! That every imperfection might be removed (v.27)!

God has called husbands to treat their wives in similar fashion. I don't know one man who would not want to remove all of his wife's 'spots' and 'wrinkles' (v.27). However, the reference is not to physical realities, but to spiritual ones. The intention is not an airbrushed version of your wife's best photograph in which all of the things she might list as imperfections are removed. This is a deeper, inner cleansing.

Husband, God has given you the authority to lovingly woo and draw out of your wife all of her potential for beauty. In an atmosphere of love and acceptance you are to call out all that stands in the way of her full development into the woman God wants her to be. Satan stands ready, however, with his counterfeits once again. We swallow his lie to attempt to change her without first accepting her. The first hint of that only causes her to withdraw in fear and rejection.

God's call is to accept her first. How much did Adam know about Eve when God brought her to him in the garden? Not a thing. But Adam was obviously pleased with what he saw! Adam did not know Eve, but he did know God. Because he knew God was good and would never do anything that would violate his goodness, Adam could rest assured that this precious gift he was now presented with was also part of God's good plan for him.

God calls us husbands to accept our wives first and then, in that atmosphere of the safety of our love, to seek to change her for her good and God's glory, not to fulfil our selfish wishes. God gives to the husband the authority to set his wife apart as beautiful to him, first and foremost, and then to ourselves. I do not know a woman who would not gladly submit to a man who is unselfishly committed to her full development and blossoming as a woman. Men, when your wife knows you are committed, not to manipulate her for your good, but in ministry for her good and God's glory, submission will rarely be a problem.

What does this mean on a practical level? It means that we must wash our wives with the Scriptures. What? Yes, bathe her in the Word of God. Remember, along the way, that washing is a gentle process. The way some men apply the Word of God to their relationships with their wives you would think they were cleaning rusty car parts with kerosene and a wire brush in the garage! We are washing our dear wives' souls in the pure Word of God. When we do so we need to consciously put ourselves on gentle cycle, take out the woolite for special fabrics and gently, consistently, lovingly pour the Word of God through and over her life.

'Oh, but my wife knows so much more about the Bible than I do!' Nobody said anything about teaching her anything. Just begin by reading the Bible together. Let the Scriptures do their work. Allow the Holy Spirit to do the application. Leave room for God to do the rinsing. You just expose her regularly to the Word of God. Try asking her questions and revealing to her your teachability and vulnerability in the process. 'As the rain and the snow come down from heaven, and do not return to it without watering the earth and making it bud and flourish ... so is my word that goes out from my mouth: It will not return to me empty, but will accomplish what I desire and achieve the purpose for which I sent it' (Isa. 55:10-11).

God has bounded his authority, delegated in the home to the husband, on another side as well. The third boundary marker for a husband's legitimate application of God's

107

authority is what we will call *stimulation*. God gives the husband authority to stimulate his wife's growth. 'In this same way, husbands ought to love their wives as their own bodies. He who loves his wife loves himself. After all, no one ever hated his own body, but he feeds and cares for it, just as Christ does the church – for we are members of his body' (Eph. 5:28-30).

God tells us that he has given husbands the authority to stimulate their wives' growth and development just as we stimulate our own body's welfare. There are two key words given to us here to describe the natural and normal care of one's body and, by extension, the care of the husband for the wife. We are told first to 'nourish' our wives as we do our own bodies. The word is primarily related to child rearing. In fact it is used again just a few verses later, 'Fathers, do not exasperate your children, instead *bring them up* in the training and instruction of the Lord' (Eph. 6:4, emphasis mine). That is to say, do not arbitrarily assert your authority, but provide a warm, secure atmosphere for their full development and maturity.

Husbands, how would an outsider evaluate the difference between the way you treat your wife and the way you treat your children? The specifics will and should differ, obviously, because you serve them and her in different roles. But does the same atmosphere of love, acceptance and growth you provide for your children and their development exist for your wife?

God also says that we 'cherish' our own bodies and that we should do the same for our wives. The word 'cherish' means to soften by keeping something warm. It was used in other writings of the day to describe the environment provided by a mother bird when she spreads her wings and lets her young find refuge under them.[8] It is a safe, tender love that we are given authority to extend to our wives.

It is time for an attitude check. How has your attitude toward your wife been lately? One of loving, tender acceptance? Is it like a greenhouse of refuge and growth in which she can grow and blossom into all her God-given potential? Or is there a bitter, toxic air to your relationship? Interestingly enough the parallel passage in Colossians 3:19 exhorts husbands to not be embittered against their wives. Does your attitude toward and relationship with your wife work like 'miracle grow' or herbicide on her growth and development?

The primary illustration used by the apostle is of how a normal, healthy male cares for his own body. This same attention should be given to our wives. Men, how many meals did you miss this week? Every time your tummy rumbled you went running for food, didn't you? I thought so. How many between-meal snacks have you eaten this week? How many of us have passed by a night's sleep this week? How many of you reading this have not bathed or showered this week (I hope you are reading this alone!)?

Get the point? Of course you have done those things. In fact you carried them out without a second thought because it is natural and normal to care for your body. God is telling us, 'Give the same tender care to your wife's welfare, growth and development.' Why? Because you are 'one flesh' (Gen. 2:24; Matt. 19:5).

Some men reading this may be ready to conclude that they just don't have it in them to be the nourishing and cherishing type. There are, however, 'things' in every man's life that he nourishes and cherishes. I have seen grown men hover over a classic car like a mother hen over her chicks. I know of men who give themselves passionately to a hobby. I've seen men give more care to a farm animal than their wives. I have seen a man make sacrifices for a career or to chase a dream that they wouldn't dream of making for the woman they are wed to.

Husbands, to what do you give your most careful and constant attention? How can you begin to prove to your wife today that she rises above even that in your commitment to her? Just as your body takes pre-eminence in your care for it, so your wife should take first place in your commitment to her growth.

Jesus again is our perfect pattern. He nourishes and cherishes us that we might become all that he has created and re-created us to be. Satan says, 'You're not getting your due here. Redirect your attention, look elsewhere, give yourself to something more fulfilling!' When we buy the lie we thrust our wives out of the safe, loving environment which we have been commissioned and endued with authority to provide her with, with the result that she takes the full weight of pressures, anxieties and problems she was never designed by God to carry.

Sacrifice, sanctification and stimulation have provided for us a three-sided boundary to understand the realm in which we as husbands can legitimately exercise God's authority in our marriages. There is a fourth boundary marker which closes the gap and brings to completion our understanding of the authority delegated to the husband – that boundary is *separation*. God grants to the husband the authority to separate himself to his wife alone. Quoting from Genesis 2:24, Paul says, 'For this reason a man will leave his father and mother and be united to his wife, and the two will become one flesh' (Eph. 5:31). While this quotation provides Old Testament authentication for all the apostle has been saying about the authority of God in marriage, it also serves to wrap up in one sentence the essence of God's design for marriage – total separation to another.

God gives the husband the authority to leave his parents and cleave to his wife. Leaving and cleaving may be the root of more marital struggles than just about anything else. Men, as you commit yourselves to your wives, what do you need to leave behind in order to make that commitment complete? Perhaps it is Mom and Dad, as suggested here by the apostle. I have found that often men are more entangled in mom's apron strings than women are. That which you must drop and walk away from to fully embrace your wife in unconditional commitment may be something else entirely. No matter what its identity, it must be left behind. God gives you the authority to exercise his power to leave those most cherished of treasures behind as you move toward your wife.

The correlating action is cleaving. Literally the word means to be glued to something. It signifies an inseparable bond. What is it, men, that keeps you from being so committed to your wife? Job? Hobby? Kids? Parents? Leisure? Friends?

There was an old wedding custom in the Netherlands which we would do well to bring back to our modern ceremonies. When a couple was married and went to their house after the wedding, they would enter the home through a special door. The door was never again used until one of the marriage partners died, then they were carried back out through that door which had never been opened since the wedding day.

God gives us husbands the authority to walk through the covenant door with our wives, shut it, lock it, and guard it to make certain that no one and no thing passes through it. This kind of commitment has been beautifully incarnated for us in the marriage of Robertson and Muriel McQuilkin. Mr. McQuilkin was for many years the president of Columbia Bible College and Seminary (now Columbia International University) in Columbia, South Carolina. Humanly speaking Mr. McQuilkin was indispensable to the growing ministry of the institution. He personally had what many would have believed to have been all a man like him could have wanted: leading an exploding ministry at the college and graduate levels, travelling the world over as one of the world's leading spokesmen on world missions, in constant demand as a Bible teacher, preacher, lecturer, and author of numerous books and articles. But then, after forty-two years of wonderful marriage, Muriel began to develop Alzheimer's Disease. The decline was slow at first and special arrangements could be made for her care while Robertson was travelling and at the office. As the disease moved into its more advanced stages, however, no one seemed able to provide the care she needed and desired except for her husband of over four decades. One day Robertson made up his mind; the decision that had to be made was clear to him – he must leave the college and seminary and personally care for his wife.

> When the time came, the decision was firm. It took no great calculation. It was a matter of integrity. Had I not promised, 42 years before, 'in sickness and in health ... till death do us part'? This was not grim duty to which I was stoically resigned, however. It was only fair. She had, after all, cared for me for almost four decades with marvelous devotion; now it was my turn. And such a partner she was! If I took care of her for 40 years, I would never be out of her debt.[9]

Gone were the extensive travels to exciting fields of evangelistic advance across the world, gone were the days of cutting edge development of kingdom servants for those mission fields, gone were the many speaking engagements. All so he could care for a woman who now could barely remember his name. Why? Why would such an enormously useful servant of God shut himself away in a little house with a woman who could not reciprocate his love and care? Because he remembered his commitments ... He had vowed to separate himself to her. Robertson McQuilkin has reminded us that the greatest ministry we will ever have for Christ is that of honouring our commitment to our wives. I suggest to you that Roberston McQuilkin understands what it is to be accountable before God as one delegated with authority to lead his home.

Mr. McQuilkin wants to hear none of the hero-talk about what he is doing. He insists it is all part of the marriage covenant.

> I have been startled by the response to the announcement of my resignation. Husbands and wives renew marriage vows, pastors tell the story to their congregations. It was a mystery to me, until a distinguished oncologist who lives constantly with dying people

told me, 'Almost all women stand by their men; very few men stand by their women.' Perhaps people sensed this contemporary tragedy and somehow were helped by a simple choice I considered the only option.[10]

What does it mean that God has delegated something of his authority to the husband? Yes, there is leadership, taking the fore on occasion, tough decisions, headship – it is all a part of being God's delegated authority in marriage. Have you noticed, however, where God spends his time in Scripture? On making certain he marks out the boundaries of that authority so that we can see the realm in which such leadership takes place. God gives the husband the authority to exercise divinely-given power in sacrificing himself for his wife, to sanctify her to God and himself, to stimulate her growth and to separate her to himself alone.

I can hear the skeptic still ask, 'Yes, but what if my husband isn't like Robertson McQuilkin?' What does Scripture say? 'Wives, in the same way be submissive to your husbands so that, if any of them do not believe the word, they may be won over without words by the behavior of their wives, when they see the purity and reverence of your lives' (1 Pet. 3:1-2).

'Oh, but what if he tells me to do something sinful?' 'What if my husband is abusive?' 'What if life is simply unlivable with him?' God alone possesses absolute authority. A husband's authority is measured, delegated, relative and limited. The husband will answer to absolute authority for his use of delegated authority. When a husband steps outside of God's design and begins to compel his wife to sinful behaviour, she must draw the line and obey Christ rather than her man. I do not believe God requires a woman to physically remain in a location where she and/or her children are likely to be physically harmed.

Sickening stories of abuse abound today. They break the heart of God even more than they do ours. Yet it seems to me that the escalation of cases of such horrible spousal abuse has brought with them another problem riding on their shirt-tail. The word 'abuse' is now applied to many situations. We hear of 'verbal abuse', 'psychological abuse', 'emotional abuse' and other strains of the sickness infecting marital relationships. The majority of people I talk to could, under today's definition, point to some kind of 'abuse' if the right word can be hyphenated in front of it.

My concern is twofold. First, we must do everything possible to wipe out the misunderstanding of delegated authority within the home and the resulting pain it causes to its victims. That is one reason I am writing this book. Second, we must ask ourselves a question. All the legitimate cases of horrible abuse notwithstanding, when we get past today's definitions and qualifications and identifications of abuse, who is left to hear God's call to wives in 1 Peter 3:1-2? Is it possible that some legitimately discontented and discouraged, but not truly abused, women have, in their pain, used the word 'abuse' as a way to get out from under God's commands to the wife? Will God's Word work in a new millennium? Or have we identified the one passage that no longer adequately embraces the true struggles of humanity?

I contend that God's Word still stands true. From a society with a traditional understanding of the home and marriage that places far more authority on the husband than does ours, comes an account to illustrate the efficacy of obedience to God's commands to wives.

Shirai was a young Japanese wife whose husband was the traditional lord of the house. When she came to faith in Christ, he was furious. If she ever went to that Christian meeting again, he warned, she would be locked out. Sunday night Shirai came home to a darkened, locked home. She slept on the doorstep till morning, and when her husband opened the door, she smiled sweetly and hurried to prepare the best possible breakfast of bean soup, rice, and raw fish. Every Sunday and every Wednesday the story was the same. Winter came, and with it the rain and cold. Shirai huddled in the darkness as her wet cotton-padded jacket froze about her.

Week after week for six months she forgave, freely and fully. No recriminations, no sulking. It was costly – she bore his sin. But her poor husband finally could stand it no longer. Love finally won out. When I met him, he was a pillar in the church, learning to walk the thorny path of sacrificial love. Shirai's example shatters my own complacency with a sharp, clear picture of what it means to deny oneself, take up one's cross daily, and follow Jesus.[11]

Obedience may not always be possible for those under the leadership of delegated authorities, but submission always is. Let us never forget the awesome power of submission when reverently wielded in Jesus' name.

NOTES

1. Not their real names.

2. Stephen Bedale, 'The Meaning of *kephale* in the Pauline Epistles', *Journal of Theological Studies* 5 (1954): 215.

3. See H. Wayne House, *The Role of Women in Ministry Today* (Grand Rapids, Michigan: Baker Book House, 1995), pp.25-33; and especially Wayne Grudem, 'Does Kephale ("Head") Mean "Source" or "Authority Over" in Greek Literature? A Survey of 2,336 Examples,' appendix I in George W. Knight III, *The Role Relationship of Men and Women* (Chicago: Moody Press, 1985), pp.49-80. Also Dr. Grudem's 'The Meaning of "Kephale ('Head'): A Response to Recent Studies"', appendix I in John Piper and Wayne Grudem, *Recovering Biblical Manhood and Womanhood* (Wheaton, Illinois: Crossway Books, 1991), pp.425-468.

4. Wayne Grudem, 'The meaning of "head" in the Bible,' in *CBMW News*, Vol.1 No. 3 (Libertyville, Illinois: Council on Biblical Manhood and Womanhood, June 1996), p.8.

5. Stephen D. Kovach, 'Egalitarians revamp the doctrine of the Trinity', in *CBMW News*, Vol.2 No. 1 (Libertyville, Illinois: Council on Biblical Manhood and Womanhood, December 1996), pp.1, 3-5.

6. Ibid.

7. Elizabeth Elliot, *The Mark of a Man* (Tarrytown, New York: Fleming H. Revell Company, 1981), p.105.

8. W. E. Vine, *Vine's Expository Dictionary of New Testament Words* (McClean, Virginia: MacDonald Publishing Company, n.d.), p.186.

9. Robertson McQuilkin, *Living By Vows* (Columbia, South Carolina: Columbia International University, n.d.).

10. Ibid.

11. Robertson McQuilkin, *An Introduction to Biblical Ethics* (Wheaton, Illinois: Tyndale House Publishers, Inc., 1995), pp.23-24.

The Authority of God and Parenthood

The idealogical fisticuffs over a divinely instituted authority structure in the home do not end when a husband and wife square off over their roles. Today even the notion of parental authority over children is distasteful to the current cultural palate. It is more popular to pursue friendship with your children than exercise loving authority. If we believe much of the popular parenthood psychology, what our children need most is a good buddy, not an environment where the loving authority of God is modelled.

No doubt the struggle begins with our innate desire to be in charge of the world – or at least our little corner of it. Young or old, rich or poor, learned or simple, everyone at some time wants their shot at the control panel of the universe.

Bill Watterson, creator of the comic strip *Calvin and Hobbs*, has expressed our desire and our demise well. In one of his four-frame comics Watterson has pictured the young boy Calvin towering over two little flowers that have sprouted from the earth. A watering can in his right hand, Calvin asks, with a congenial look upon his face, 'So you want some water, huh? Well, I've got a big can of it here.' The second frame reveals that Calvin's countenance has changed. The watering can has now been set aside. One hand on his hip and the other pumping his thumb in a motion toward himself, Calvin's expression is defiant: 'It's up to ME to decide if you get water or not! I control your fate! Your very LIVES are in my hands!' Frame three reveals that Calvin's intensity has only increased. He now rails in a thunderous voice like a doomsday prophet: 'Without ME you're as good as dead! Without ME, you don't...' Frame four shows Calvin standing with slumped shoulders, a chagrined look upon his face. The corners of his mouth have turned downward, for he, his tiny watering can and the two flowers are being overwhelmed by a torrential downpour from heaven!

Don't we all, at times, long to be able to arrange the circumstances of life to conform to our preferences? Frankly we would not do a very good job of it. No matter what our age, we humans simply are not cut out for such lofty work. Sovereignty is too heavy and cumbersome a load for hands of finitude; God alone is able to wield sovereignty. Even if he were to let us try our hand at sovereignty, the power surge of ultimate authority would blow our circuitry. We simply are not able. For that reason God keeps the reins of the universe in his own hands. In my best moments I am profoundly thankful for that; in moments of lesser insight I still think I might have done things a bit differently.

Yet, as we have seen, in his administration of his creation, God has delegated some of his authority to certain channels within that creation. God has delegated measured portions of his authority in order that his orderly, divine plan might be worked out in our actual experience. We have traced how God has delegated a limited portion of his authority to the governing authorities and, in an entirely different realm, also to the leadership of the local church. Yet God has become even more personal in the delegation of authority. Few of us have direct access to the governing authorities. In the West we have the right to representation and a voice in the governing of our land. For this we are thankful. But the day to day decision-making of those in places of governmental leadership is at least one step removed from the daily flow of our lives. The church is certainly a great deal closer to home. Yet even here some may choose not to be as intimately involved in the actual fellowship, ministry, and life of a local church as God has designed. We have many excuses for avoiding authority. God, however, has extended the arm of his delegated authority so that none of us can completely avoid it – he has delegated his authority into the leadership of the home. We must come to see this as part of his working out of his perfect plan for our lives. We may for a given moment, or perhaps even an extended season, wonder about God's methods, but we must in the end come to see God's wisdom in delegating a measure of his authority within the home.

God has built his universe to function under his authority. To live in his world is to be confronted by his authority. What better place to learn a healthy view of and response to authority than in the home during our earliest days? How many of our current problems could be averted if only lessons of authority and submission were learned in the healthy, safe and loving environment of the home? If a child does not learn to respond in appropriate ways to the authority of God delegated to his parents, he will learn it somewhere else. Perhaps it will be a teacher who will drive home the lesson. It may be that the lesson of authority and the appropriate response to it will come at the hands of an employer who has had enough of their attitude. Perhaps it could be a law enforcement officer and the legal system that will be pressed into service to make the lessons of authority clear. If all delegated authorities fail to break through to the individual, after a life of fighting and struggle, the child will finally stand before the unveiled and absolute authority of God himself. We will never escape the issue of authority. Where better to learn it than at home, under the gentle but firm care of wise parents?

Unfortunately recent days have seen a formalization of the assault on the authority of the home. A growing children's rights movement seeks to provide children the same legal rights in court as their parents enjoy. Sounds benign enough, until the goal of children being allowed legal grounds to sue their parents for divorce is exposed. In a highly publicized case, that is exactly what twelve-year-old Gregory Kingsley of Orlando, Florida did when he took his mother to court and sued to legally separate himself from her. In somewhat similar fashion child film star Macaulay Culkin, of the *Home Alone* films, went to court to protect his millions from his parents.

The legal angles for children fed up with parents seems to be broadening more all the time. In 1989 the United Nations held their Convention of the Child in which a treaty was signed by more than 140 nations. The charter contains 54 points, among which is the provision to protect children from 'all forms of discrimination or punishment on the basis of status, activities, expressed opinions or beliefs of the child's parents'.[1]

Let me state something clearly from the beginning. There are some parents who are horrible at their job. The accounts of child abuse grow more sickening by the day. Recently our local news broadcasts have told of parents who routinely locked their eight-year-old daughter in a dog cage in the basement each day after she arrived home from school and kept her there until it was time to leave for class again the next morning. She was only rescued when her older brother fled the home to local police officials who then came to her aid. Such parents should be punished. Such children should be protected. Abuse of a child is of the most heinous of sins. Yet, in our denunciations, let us be careful about our definitions. Biblical discipline of a child, even corporeal discipline, is not the same as abuse. Charles Swindoll provides a helpful list of distinctions between abuse and biblical discipline.

Abuse	*Discipline*
Unfair and unexpected	Fair and expected
Degrading and demoralizing	Upholds dignity
Extreme – too harsh, brutal	Balanced – within limits
Torturous – leaves scars	Painful – but leaves no scars
Results from hatred and resentment	Prompted by love and concern
Creates terror, emotional damage, and resentment of authority	Leads to healthy respect of and for authority
Destroys self-esteem; leads to horrifying, permanent damage and the inability, later in life, to maintain responsibilities[2]	Strengthens self-esteem; leads to the individual's ability to later discipline himself

Ultimately the question must be answered. What are the legitimate, God-given bounds of authority for parents over their children? Clearly Scripture imposes some limits upon parental authority. Why else would Paul say, 'Fathers, do not exasperate your children; instead, bring them up in the training and instruction of the Lord' (Eph. 6:4)? Before we can answer the question of the bounds of parental authority, we must answer the question of the purpose of God's giving authority to them in the first place. Why has God so orchestrated the universe that parents are in authority over their children? No better source for an answer may be found than the ancient wisdom of the Proverbs. Here we discover that God has given authority to parents so that they may cooperate with him in producing an adult full of biblical wisdom. At least ten times in the Book of Proverbs God speaks of a 'wise son' being his goal. Take a sample from this selection: 'My son, pay attention to wisdom' (5:1). 'A wise son brings joy to his father' (10:1; 15:20). 'A wise son heeds his father's instruction' (13:1). 'My son, if your heart is wise, then my heart will be glad' (23:15). 'Listen, my son, and be wise' (23:19). 'He who has a wise son delights in him' (23:24). 'Be wise, my son, and bring joy to my heart' (27:11).

Just what is the wisdom to which God and the parents are aiming in their cooperative effort in the child's life? 'In the Book of Proverbs "wisdom" signifies skillful living – the ability to make wise choices and live successfully according to the moral standards of the covenant community. The one who lives skillfully produces things of lasting value to God and to the community.'[3] God has invested his authority in parents so that through them he may bring forth a wise individual capable of living in God's world in harmony with him and the people he has created in such a way that their lives matter for eternity.

More specifically Proverbs tells us that a wise child is one who possesses qualities such as discernment, understanding, knowledge, discretion, and the fear of the Lord. The wise person has discernment – the ability to distinguish between options, events, happenings, people and ideas, and to take that perception to the next step of an understanding, wise response.[4] This insight for wise living is rooted in only one source: 'the knowledge of the Holy One is understanding' (Prov. 9:10). 'Discretion' is also found among the sharp arrows in wisdom's quiver (Prov. 1:4; 2:11; 3:21; 5:2). The root of the word speaks of plotting and scheming – often of evil men's plans. But the singular form is employed in a positive way in the Proverbs to speak of the wise man's ability to think, plan, reason, prepare, and execute wise plans that honour God and bring about his ends.[5] Certainly the wise man presented to us in Proverbs is one who understands the fear of the Lord (8:13; 9:10; 10:27; 14:16-17). The wise individual is one who rightly understands the authority of God and renders appropriate awe-filled submission. A wise child is one who can hear and heed the voice of God as it comes through genuine earthly authorities (4:1). The wise person, in short, relates well to the ultimate authority of God himself and to the delegated authorities he has placed in his life.

Using these various brushes God paints a portrait of the wise person he has in mind as he entrusts parents with his authority. The question arises, what does the parent have authority to do in order to cooperate with God in seeing this happen in the life of their child? Proverbs gives numerous words that describe the means God uses to make us wise. God as our Father models for earthly, human parents how to cooperate with him in the venture of establishing children as wise adults who can live in God's world to his glory.

A number of words stand out as we observe from Proverbs how it is God works to bring us to wisdom – words like counsel, reproof, commandments, laws, sayings, teaching, instruction and words. All of these describe the means and methods of God in moving us from foolishness and folly to wisdom. They also apply to the things God has given parents authority to do to cooperate with him in bringing their children to wisdom.

'Counsel' (*y'ṣ*) is a Hebrew word that indicates both a predetermined plan and the advice given to those who are to come into conformity with that plan.[6] We are told of 'the counsels of the Lord' (Prov. 19:21; Ps. 33:11). God has a course of events which all of history is to follow and over which he sovereignly sits, working it to his own ultimate glory. Thus the whole world, all of history, every life – from creation to the establishment of the eternal state – is designed to fit God's plan. Hence we are told that man's plans will ultimately fail (Isa. 14:24-27), but God's counsels will stand forever (Ps. 33:10-11). Thus in the specifics of our individual experiences God counsels us to bring our lives into harmony with the flow of history as he is working it out to his purposes. To accept and heed this advice from God is a mark of the wise person.

This is one way our heavenly Father parents us toward wisdom. Earthly parents, employing delegated authority, have the authority to set a course of right conduct and behaviour for their children. The standards of behaviour should not be arbitrarily set, but rather established to help bring the child's life in line with God's overall purposes and aid them in becoming a part of what God is doing to promote his own glory. With the authority to establish right standards of conduct, the parents then can authoritatively counsel their children to follow these established paths. This would mean not merely 'laying down the law', but helping bring the child along in understanding the purposes of the Lord and how their behaviour can promote those purposes. Interestingly, the Hebrew word translated 'counsel' is the same word found in the Messianic anticipation of Jesus Christ when he is called 'Wonderful Counselor' (Isa. 9:6). Similarly the Holy Spirit is called 'the Spirit of counsel' (Isa. 11:2). 'The child who is to come, on whose shoulders the government of the world shall rest, is one whose plans, purposes, designs and decrees for his people are marvelous.'[7] Thus parents not only have the authority but the obligation to so counsel their child that he will come to know Jesus Christ personally, and walk submissively under his counsel. Likewise the parents have the authority to train their child to be responsive personally to the inner counsel of the Spirit of God as he nudges him toward God's ways.

The word 'reproof' (*yākaḥ*) is another word frequently found in the Book of Proverbs in conjunction with God's attempts to bring us to wisdom. The root form of the word indicates that a judicial, forensic kind of rebuke is often implied. One who has the right of judgement brings official censure to another's wrong or inappropriate actions. There is, however, a sense of instruction and teaching to the word as well.[8] God does not just 'lower the boom' on us, he uses all means of rebuke to educate and point us to a fuller understanding of his ways, purposes and sovereign plans and how we can work with him to his glory.

Another Hebrew word, *mûsār* ('instruction'), is also employed with a similar meaning. God uses this to describe correction which results in learning. This discipline may at times be difficult, but should not be understood negatively, for God always balances the hardships of his discipline with the miracles of his provision. Such was the case in the wilderness wanderings where God disciplined the children of Israel, but provided food, water and other provisions throughout the experience. This was done 'to teach you that man does not live on bread alone but on every word that comes out of the mouth of the LORD. Your clothes did not wear out and your feet did not swell during these forty years. Know then in your heart that as a man disciplines his son, so the Lord your God disciplines you' (Deut. 8:3b-5). Primarily this discipline is understood to be verbal.[9]

The parallel application to our parenting authority would indicate that parents have God-given authority to both re-enforce appropriate behaviour and censure inappropriate behaviour by words and even actions of rebuke. These words and any resultant actions of reproof must not be merely punishment, but so crafted and administered as to have an educational effect upon the child. Rebuke should be employed with love to help the child learn the right path that is both safe and honouring to God.

God also issues 'commandments' to move us, his children, toward wise living. Here is used not only the more common Hebrew word *ṯôrâ*, but also the word *miṣwâ*. The former is most often translated by our word law, while the latter has our idea of commandment. 'It reflects a firmly structured society in which people were responsible to their right to rule by God's command.'[10] God's commandments are clearly made known and communicated to his people (Deut. 30:11). They are found to be pure (Ps. 19:8), true (119:151), reliable (119:86), and righteous (119:172). Blessing follows upon obedience to them and discipline upon disobedience (Deut. 11:26ff).[11]

Parents are invested with measured authority by God to bring about wisdom in their children. To this end they have the prerogative to establish 'do's' and 'don'ts'. Parents do not speak with supreme authority, but only delegated authority. Nevertheless they can speak with firmness and enforce their rules with consequences. Consequences should not be only negative for disobedience, but a watchful eye must be kept to render positive blessing for obedience to their commands. Parents must not assume their will is understood, but must work to clearly establish the ground rules of the home with their children. Once these are clearly communicated and understood, the parent has the authority to enforce these rules.

The Book of Proverbs also employs the terms 'sayings' and 'words' to show us how God moves us as his children toward wisdom. The Hebrew word translated 'saying' is from the root *'āmar*, which appears over five thousand times in the Old Testament. It is the most common way to speak of communicating with words. Similarly we find in Proverbs God's 'words' (*dābār*) used in his efforts to build wisdom into us. This common Hebrew root is used often and is so rich in its meaning that the King James Version translators employed over eighty-five different ways of rendering it.[12] Parents need to talk to their children – all the time, in every conceivable circumstance, under every condition. We must communicate! We are not to talk *at* our children but talk *with* and *to* our children. Every word we speak should be designed to move our children toward wisely living for God. These will include words of love, affirmation, correction, instruction, reproof, commitment, comfort, counsel and command. Every time a parent opens his mouth he is wielding perhaps their most weighty tool in sculpting his child for God's purposes. We must speak with care and intention.

We have stopped to look more closely at what the Book of Proverbs says to us about how God the Father parents us toward wisdom, looking for parallels to how we may cooperate with him in moving our children toward the same goal. Do you notice what all these words have in common? They all have to do with *relationship*. Parents most definitely have been endued by God with authority to raise their children. That authority is to be employed for the purposes of preparing a young adult who is filled with wisdom and knows how to live in God's world in harmony with God and his creation. That goal will be arrived at only as parents intentionally prioritize and pursue an ever-deepening relationship with their children. We will never produce disciples of Jesus Christ with part-time parenting. The raising of our children will require every ounce of energy, every drop of wisdom, every penny of provision that God can pour through our lives. Parenthood is impossible without God! But, oh, the glorious privilege of being God's tool to craft a fully devoted follower of Jesus and to be used by him to deploy them into the world for God's strategic purposes! There is no higher calling.

To arrive at this glorious goal parents have then the authority to employ words, counsel, structures, rules, guidelines, reproof and instruction in their calling to bring forth children who possesses discernment, understanding, knowledge, discretion and the fear of the Lord.

I hear a skeptic in the crowd: 'Ah, but doesn't Proverbs talk about "the rod" also?' Yes, the Bible speaks of corporeal discipline (spanking, if you will) as another appropriate tool to be employed in this glorious vocation of parenthood. I have saved our discussion of 'the rod' till now because too often that is all some remember about discipline from the Bible. For this reason I have focused first on the larger understanding of discipline. Make no mistake, however, the Scriptures do make provision for corporeal discipline. Let's examine what the Book says about this.

Some object to the idea of spanking because, if they have listened to much of the popular thinking in this area, they feel it is cruel. Quite the opposite is the case, however. 'He who spares the rod hates his son, but he who loves him is careful to discipline him' (Prov. 13:24). Others believe that corporeal punishment could possibly leave permanent emotional scars upon the child that will adversely affect them later in life. Wrong again. Appropriately applied corporeal punishment protects the child later in life. 'Do not withhold discipline from a child; if you punish him with the rod, he will not die. Punish him with the rod and save his soul from death' (Prov. 23:13-14). The child, left to his childishness, will only run downhill ... and at the bottom of the hill is an abrupt stop called 'death'.

The matter of discipline will not be settled by merely examining the methods employed, or even the projected outcome of those methods. The matter of discipline, biblically speaking, starts with the child himself. What is really in that car seat that comes home from the hospital? That little bundle of joy comes with more than joy bundled amidst those pastel-coloured blankets. 'Folly is bound up in the heart of a child, but the rod of discipline will drive it far from him' (Prov. 22:15). Foolishness, by the definition of the writer of Proverbs, is moral impertinence. It is the natural course of a child to be insolent and impertinent. That is why the word 'child' is found in childishness. Corporeal discipline is one of the tools given the parent by God to cooperate with him in bringing the child from foolishness to wisdom. It is the one that is most specifically mentioned as the remedy for the foolishness of our hearts. 'The rod of correction imparts wisdom, but a child left to himself disgraces his mother' (Prov. 29:15).

It is reported that the British poet Samuel Taylor Coleridge had occasion to entertain a man who was confirmed in his belief that children should never be given any formal religious training. Rather, he felt, they should have the liberty to choose their own spiritual direction later in life. The poet avoided a confrontation as the man espoused his view with conviction. Later, however, he led the gentleman out of doors and showed him his garden – full of weeds and in desperate need of care. The visitor rebuffed Mr. Coleridge, 'Do you call this a garden? There are nothing but weeds here!' 'Well, you see,' Coleridge retorted, 'I did not wish to infringe upon the liberty of the garden in any way. I was just giving the garden a chance to express itself.'

None of us, left to ourself, will ever end up with wisdom. We begin in foolishness and folly. Without the loving discipline and guidance of wise parents we are caught in the downward vortex of our own sinful nature. What looks like the autonomy of selfhood moves downward from plain simpleness (*petî*), to foolishness and folly (*kesîl*). From here the fool, left to himself, falls even deeper into a more serious foolishness (*'ĕwîl*), and from there he descends to an even denser state of folly (*nābāl*). The vortex's power eventually pulls the foolish down to the level of what the Proverbs call a 'scoffer' (*lēṣ*).[13]

Think with me for a moment about this descent into depravity. The 'simple' (*petî*) are those who are gullible, silly and naive (14:15; 22:3). They love to exercise their wilfulness and act irresponsibly (1:32). They tend to be thoughtless toward others (19:25). Indeed their folly is a source of pleasure to them (15:21). They waste their life chasing after what does not matter (15:21). We all begin in the naiveté of the simple.

Left undirected and unrestrained the power of the vortex begins the downward tug of rebellion that will destroy our lives (22:3). At this stage the simple are still reachable and able to be rescued from the current of their foolishness (19:25).[14]

The 'fool' (*kesîl*) is the next downward step for the simpleton who refuses to learn. This is the most common term referring to the fool in Proverbs. It indicates one who is thick-headed and stubborn. It is not that the fool is stupid, but rather that he has, by his refusal to listen to the wisdom of his parents, chosen a resolute outlook on life. The source of his problem is spiritual, not a mental deficiency. He has no place for truth in his life and no time for the fear of the Lord (14:8; 1:29). The *kesîl* brings agony, bitterness and catastrophe to his parents (10:1; 17:21; 17:25; 19:13). Not only does he bring his parents ruin, he despises them (15:20).[15]

Without parental restraint and serious intervention the *kesîl* moves downward further to the level of the *'ĕwîl*. The *'ĕwîl* shares many of the same characteristics of the *kesîl*, only his moral insolence is taken even further. He refuses counsel (1:7; 10:8; 12:15; 15:15) and mocks at sin (14:9). Unless this kind of attitude and behaviour is corrected early in life the downward pull of the vortex can become nearly irreversible (22:15; 27:22).[16]

There is, however, another step down for the fool. From the derision of the *'ĕwîl* he falls to the level of the *nābāl*. Again sharing many of the same character traits of the *kesîl* and *'ĕwîl*, the *nābāl* goes even further by closing his mind completely to God (Ps. 14:1). The godless *nābāl* is illustrated for us by the husband of Abigail (1 Sam. 25:25) whose own name was Nabal. Of him, his own wife confessed that 'one cannot speak to him' (25:17).[17]

Finally, the furthest level of descent described in Proverbs is that of the 'scoffer' (*leṣ*). The scoffer despises being amended in his actions or thinking (9:7, 8; 13:1; 15:12). His independence makes movement toward wisdom impossible (14:6). The scoffer is no longer a simpleton who curiously investigates folly here and there, but is one who has become confirmed in his reviling of all authority (21:24; 22:10; 29:8). The sad verdict awaiting the scoffer is that the God whom he has scoffed will in the end return the favour back upon his head (3:34).[18]

This downward spiral of autonomy leads the child to death (Prov. 19:18) and delivers the parent into shame (29:15). Any parent wants to spare their child this kind of existence as well as protect themselves from the pain of sharing life with such a child. Fortunately Scripture prescribes clear guidance on how to discipline early so as to avoid the folly of foolishness. Proverbs provides a number of parameters within which the parental authority to exercise discipline must take place. Our discipline must be fair. All that we have already discovered about discipline in Proverbs compels us to clear communication. To place unspoken expectations upon our children is neither fair nor God-honouring. We must talk, reason, explain, instruct and reprove. 'Fathers, do not exasperate your children; instead, bring them up in the training and instruction of the Lord' (Eph. 6:4). 'Fathers, do not embitter your children, or they will become discouraged' (Col. 3:21). Unfair and unspoken expectations only defeat a child.

Our discipline must not only be fair, it must be firm. When the boundaries have been clearly established and what is acceptable and unacceptable has been made clear, then defiance must not be tolerated. Defiance is the time for corporeal punishment. Remember here all that was said earlier about the difference between discipline and abuse. I am not advocating the latter, but I am exhorting us never to abandon the former because of cultural misunderstandings. Hollow threats and repeated warnings without follow-through only train our children that we do not mean what we say and that we should not be taken seriously.

Our discipline must also be consistent. Start early, keep at it. 'Discipline your son, for in that there is hope' (Prov. 19:18). Though there are times in the trials of parenthood that throwing up your arms, turning your back, putting the headphones on and turning the volume up seems the more pleasant option than dealing AGAIN with your child – it is only despair dressed up like momentary relief. Start early! 'Discipline your son while there is hope' (NASB). Keep at it! Your children need the security of knowing what to expect. Training them to conclude that you do not mean what you say (by hollow threats of discipline) and then eventually flying off in a rage of severe and harsh retribution does not promote wisdom in their hearts.

Parents, God has delegated to you a measure of his authority to discipline your children. Please note, however, the difference between punishment and discipline. Betty Chase has helpfully clarified the two for us. The purpose of punishment is to inflict penalty for an offence, while the purpose of discipline is to train for correction and maturity. The focus of punishment is past misdeeds, while discipline focuses on future correct deeds. The attitude of punishment is hostility and frustration on the part of the parent, while discipline is administered with an attitude of love and concern on the part of the parent. The emotions that result in a child who faces punishment are fear and guilt, while after loving discipline they discover a sense of security.[19]

Proverbs holds out punishment as that which is appropriate for the wicked (10:16), those who are confirmed in their evil and rebellion toward God. On the other hand, loving discipline is the order of the day for the foolishness and folly of a child.

What has God given parents the authority to do? Remember the goal! God has called parents to cooperate with him in developing a wise adult, an adult who loves God fully and expresses that devotion through obedient submission to him and those he has placed over him. God has given parents the authority to engage any and all of the forms of discipline we have discovered in Proverbs in order to move their child to this place of discipleship.

The authority of a parent is unique among all God's

delegated authorities. The authority of parenthood is designed from the beginning to work until it makes itself unnecessary. At some point the relationship of parent and child makes a transition. There comes a turning point when the child moves out from under the authority of their parents and functions as an adult under God's direct authority. A child never outgrows his responsibility to honour his parents. But he does, in God's design, grow to a place where he no longer functions under the direct authority of his parents. Children never outgrow the need of, or obligation to authority, but they do reach the place where the delegated authority of their parents is no longer as central to their lives.

When does that moment of transition occur? We are not told specifically. There is no magic age, no universally identifiable sign that the time has arrived. The question of timing is probably best answered by looking once again at the purpose of the parent's authority. Parents are invested with authority in order to raise a wise child. In the exercise of that authority there comes a point (like it or not) when it is the child's turn to evidence the wisdom the parents have modelled, prayed for, and worked to instil. There comes a time when the parent's hands are pulled back and the man himself must show forth his own position with regard to wisdom (Prov. 29:3a; 2:2ff). Charles Swindoll has given helpful counsel to anxious parents.

> We are to model God's place of authority until our children are sufficiently mature to shift the authority from us to their heavenly Parent. Beyond that transitional time, parents, take your hands off! You are dealing with an adult at that point, not a child, so don't treat him like a child. Release him.
>
> If it's off to college, release your grip. If it's marriage, release him to marriage. If it's his own career, fine; let him pursue that career. Respect his God-appointed right to grow up.
>
> Model God's role of authority until the children reach the place where there is a natural shift of authority, then let 'em go!'[20]

Perhaps it could be said that the structures of a parent's authority are not unlike some sutures that doctors use in the repair of our bodies. In some parts of our body the healing process is best served by the use of stitches that naturally dissolve on their own. Like those sutures a parent's authority is given by God to hold things together so that wholeness can take place, but they are necessary only for a time. Wholeness is expected from the beginning. It is painful to let go – 'What if her life comes apart!' Yet, if a wise, whole disciple of Jesus Christ is ever to be deployed into the world that moment of letting go must come. May we trust God to give us wisdom to hold them together until its time to trust him for the grace to let them go.

NOTES

1. Randy Frame, 'Child vs. Parent', *Christianity Today*, March 7, 1994, pp.42-43.

2. Charles Swindoll, *The Strong Family* (Grand Rapids, Michigan: Zondervan Publishing House, 1991), p.94.

3. Allen P. Ross, 'Proverbs', *The Expositor's Bible Commentary*, v.5 (Zondervan Publishing House, 1991), p.905.

4. Louis Goldberg, *bîn*, *Theological Wordbook of the Old Testament*, v.1 (Chicago: Moody Press, 1980), p.103.

5. Herbert Wolf, *zāmam*, *Theological Wordbook of the Old Testament*, v.1 (Chicago: Moody Press, 1980), p.244.

6. Al Wolters, *New International Dictionary of Old Testament Theology and Exegesis*, v.2 (Grand Rapids, Michigan: Zondervan Publishing House, 1997), pp.490-492.

7. Paul R. Gilchrist, *ya'as*, *Theological Wordbook of the Old Testament*, v.1 (Chicago: Moody Press, 1980), p.391.

8. Paul R. Gilchrist, *yākah*, *Theological Wordbook of the Old Testament*, v.1 (Chicago: Moody Press, 1980), pp.376-377.

9. Paul R. Gilchrist, *yāsar*, *Theological Wordbook of the Old Testament*, v.1 (Chicago: Moody Press, 1980), pp.386-387.

10. A. H. Konkel, *ṣāwâ*, *Theological Wordbook of the Old Testament*, v.2 (Chicago: Moody Press, 1980), p.757.

11. Ibid.

12. Earl S. Kalland, *dābār*, *Theological Wordbook of the Old Testament*, v.1, (Chicago: Moody Press, 1980), p.180.

13. Derek Kidner, *Proverbs*, (Downers Grove, Illinois: Inter-Varsity Press, 1964), pp.39-42. As well as Louis Goldberg, *'wl*, *Theological Wordbook of the Old Testament*, v.1, (Chicago: Moody Press, 1980), pp.19-20.

14. Kidner, p.39.

15. Ibid., pp.40-41.

16. Ibid., p.41.

17. Ibid.

18. Ibid., pp.41-42.

19. Betty N. Chase, *How to Discipline and Build Self-Esteem in Your Child* (Elgin, Illinois: David C. Cook Publishing Company, 1982), p.12.

20. Charles R. Swindoll, *The Strong Family* (Grand Rapids, Michigan: Zondervan Publishing House, 1991), pp.107-108.

Chapter 8

The Authority of God and the Believer

By now you may be feeling like the world's doormat. No one enjoys being the low rung on the ladder. Comedian Rodney Dangerfield has made millions being the guy who 'don't get no respect'. His success is probably attributable to the fact that most of us feel we can identify with him.

Are you beginning to feel like the gum on the bottom of everyone else's shoes? Perhaps it appears as though everyone else but you has a position in which they serve in some role of delegated authority. 'What's left for me? Where do I fit in God's scheme of authority? I submit to God. I am joyfully and willingly submissive to the delegated authorities he has placed in my life. But is that it? Do I just get walked on?' Absolutely not! In this chapter I want us to consider what may be one of the most overlooked doctrines of the Bible among Western Christians – the doctrine of the authority of the believer.

With the introduction of Enlightenment thinking into our western culture the recognition of supernatural, spiritual realities began to be looked upon as fodder only for the ignorant and unlearned. Feeling that we may have lost respect in the eyes of a scholarly world, we evangelicals made a needed effort at bringing an intellectual legitimacy to our message. But with our thrust toward scholarship we may have temporarily lost a functional awareness of the supernatural, spiritual battle that rages around us. Fortunately, in the last decade we evangelicals have begun to recover at our grass roots an understanding of what many call 'spiritual warfare'. Central to a biblical understanding of spiritual warfare is the comprehension of the authority of the believer.

Are you obsessed with and paralyzed by fears that seem to have no specific object? Do consuming thoughts distress and control you? Are you overwhelmed by a seeming lack of strength to overcome temptation? Are you entangled in a web of compulsive behaviors that you are powerless to break free from? It could be that you are unaware of the authority that God has given you as a child of God; authority to be done with these intimidations of the evil one. Sometimes well-meaning children of God have believed the lie that a call to humility and meekness means that one must passively endure such struggles. I invite you to ponder with me the authority that is ours as believers in Jesus Christ.

> The seventy-two returned with joy and said, 'Lord, even the demons submit to us in your name.' He replied, 'I saw Satan fall like lightening from heaven. I have given you authority to trample upon snakes and scorpions, and to overcome all the power of the enemy; nothing will harm you. However, do not rejoice that the spirits submit to you, but rejoice that your names are written in heaven' (Luke 10:17-20).

With this account the Holy Spirit has left us key instructions concerning the authority every child of God has been given through Christ. The availability of this authority is not dependent upon the length of time a person has known Christ. It is ours by position in Christ, not by tenure of faith. The exercise of this authority depends upon the understanding of the truths of our position in Christ. When those truths are understood, appropriated and applied by faith, even the neophyte in Christ can stand victoriously against the intimidations and tactics of the evil one.

Such authority takes us by surprise. You come to Christ in recognition of your weakness, inability and need and in appreciation of his strength, ability and sufficiency. We come aware of our need of forgiveness; once we arrive we are amazed that the atonement provided by our Savior provides not only forgiveness and release from guilt, but also power to live above sin and Satan and the world. Every blood-bought child of God has been given, by virtue of Christ's finished work, the authority to apply the truth of his victory by the power of the Holy Spirit to the fulfilment of his will in our lives. What is to his followers a surprising authority, is of course no surprise to our Savior. 'The seventy-two returned with joy and said, "Lord, even the demons submit to us in your name"' (Luke 10:17). The original band sent out by our Lord to announce the coming of God's kingdom apparently did not expect their ministry assignment to meet with such success. Did they go forth with a defeatist attitude not unlike the view of ministry often adopted today? 'I'll do his will. I'll fulfill his assignment. I know it won't work. Probably nothing will happen, but I'll be faithful. After all, that is all he asks of me.'

Too many believers walk about like spiritual Eeyores. You remember Eeyore don't you? He is the gloomy, stuffed donkey of Winnie the Pooh fame. He walks through life with a dark rain cloud that hovers over him even when the sun is shining on everyone else. His gloom is self-imposed. He has a set disposition that determines defeat before the first step is taken. A good many of the believers I meet face the struggles of life with much the same sense of resignation. 'Life stinks. It always has, it always will!,' they whine. 'Jesus loves me,' they mumble with down-turned mouth, 'and praise the Lord, someday I'll get to heaven. But for now I will just hang on and get by.'

What a shock to the saints to discover that the Lord of the universe has delegated his authority to them, every one of them. Stunned saints wonder aloud, 'You mean there are spiritual struggles in my life that I do not have to put up with? Are you telling me that I may be enduring the intimidations, accusations, and attacks of the evil one and I don't have to?' Such is the surprise of the authority of the believer. God does not wish for you to be bullied by Satan and his hordes.

When I was in second grade my sister and I rode the bus to and from school every day. I was assigned a seat near the front, the older kids were in the back. In the seat in front of me was a little kindergartner. He had it in for me. I had been taught by my parents that you do not fight. So when this scrawny little kid started pushing and punching, I, remembering my parent's words, did not retaliate. I tried to block his blows, but I figured because of my parent's instructions I was destined to spend the rest of the second grade being humiliated by a kindergartner. I was bigger than him, I could have put a stop to it from the first moment. But that had never entered my mind, because I assumed that was not within the realm of my options. After this had gone on for some time my parents caught wind of what was happening each day. They sat me down and praised me for obeying them and not wanting to fight. They also, however, explained to me that I did not have to be bullied by a kindergartner! I could not believe my ears! The thought never crossed my mind that I could do something about my problem. The next day I settled it. That skinny little kid never bothered me again.

Let's be careful what implications we draw from this illustration – both for the authority of the believer and for resolving interpersonal problems. But realize that many of us reading these pages right now have subconsciously accepted a defeatist attitude toward life and are as surprised as the original disciples to learn that God has delegated his authority to us.

Our surprise quickly turns to query, 'What is this authority and where do I get it?' Jesus' words, 'I have given you authority' (Luke 10:18), point out the source of our authority. The source of the believer's authority is Jesus Christ himself. We have not the inherent power to stand against the enemy. Nor do we possess within ourselves the authority to call him to account. Jesus Christ alone is authority; graciously he has delegated his authority to his people.

This delegation of authority from Christ to his people is nowhere more beautifully taught than in the first two chapters of the letter to the Ephesians. The key phrase of this marvelous letter is 'in Christ'. Some forty times you find this phrase or concept within the pages of this one letter. Notice its prominence in the opening chapter (1:1, 3, 4, 7, 9, 11, 13). On the heels of this emphasis Paul breaks forth into prayer beginning in verse 14: 'I pray also that the eyes of your heart may be enlightened in order that you may know the hope to which he has called you, the riches of his glorious inheritance in the saints, and his incomparably great power for us who believe' (vv.18-19). You will note that the apostle has prayed that they might know three things: their hope, the inheritance God has in them, and God's great power for them as believers. Can you imagine how radically different our outlook on life would be if we possessed those three things in full measure?

Not resting content with this majestic intercession, Paul picks up on the last of the three things he prayed for, their deeper knowledge of God's power for them, and now describes that power more completely. 'That power is like the working of his mighty strength, which he exerted in Christ when he raised him from the dead and seated him at his right hand in heavenly realms, far above all rule and authority, power and dominion, and every title that can be given, not only in the present age but also in the one to come' (vv.19b-21). Employing four different Greek words in verses 19-20 to describe the awesome nature of God's power exerted in raising Jesus Christ from the dead, Paul tells us that that same power is now directed from heaven to and through us who are in Christ. In the loftiest manner possible Jesus' exaltation to the authoritative right hand of God is described: 'And God placed all things under his feet and appointed him to be head over everything for the church, which is his body, the fullness of him who fills everything in every way' (vv.22-23).

Let's take inventory of what we have discovered. The Father exerted his power in unparalleled fashion in raising Jesus from the dead and seating him at his own right hand. Jesus now sits on the seat of authority over the universe. Every opponent is now under Jesus' feet (the words 'all rule and authority, power and dominion, and every title that can be given' are references to various angelic beings, whether benevolent or malevolent). Jesus Christ is in supreme authority. 'All authority in heaven and on earth has been given to me' (Matt. 28:18). 'I looked, and there before me was one like a son of man, coming with the clouds of heaven. He approached the Ancient of Days and was led into his presence. He was given authority, glory and sovereign power; all peoples, nations and men of every language worshiped him. His dominion is an everlasting dominion that will not pass away, and his kingdom is one that will never be destroyed' (Dan. 7:13-14). There is but one throne, and Jesus is on it!

This awesome One who wields all authority has been appointed by the Father as 'head over everything *for the church*' (Eph. 1:22, emphasis mine). Did you catch that? Jesus is not named here as Head of the church, though he certainly is that. He is named as head over everything, and for what reason? For the church! Drink that in for a moment.

With Christ as head, we are then called his body, 'the fulness of him who fills everything in every way' (Eph. 1:23). A higher calling cannot be imagined than to be called to live together in such a way that we are the very body of Christ, moving as one man, accomplishing the will of our one Head. He who is our head 'fills everything in every way' – no rival will stand, no rebel will go unbowed.

How then can God make fallen humans like you and me to fulfill such a lofty calling? Little wonder Paul prayed that we might understand more deeply his magnificent power directed toward us! In his next breath the apostle begins to plumb the depths of how that magnificent power of God has set us in a position to be able to fulfill his will. He first reviews the wretchedness of our past condition (2:1-3) and then describes the miraculous transformation God has wrought in us (2:4-10).

'As for you, you were dead in your transgressions and sins' (2:1). What follows in the next two verses serves to expand upon the details of our spiritual deadness – entangled helplessly in the world system, enslaved to Satan, engrossed in the fulfillment of our own fleshly appetites, endangered by the terrifying fear of God's wrath. Then come the greatest two words in the Bible, 'But God' (v.4). With that adversative, God shows the complete transformation of nature and state he has worked in us. This came about through three actions taken by God toward us. In order to highlight the point Paul is making, allow me to take the primary clauses and piece them together without the subordinate clauses. 'You were dead in your transgressions and sins ... But ... God ... *made us alive* with Christ ... And God *raised us up* with Christ and *seated us with him* in the heavenly realms in Christ Jesus' (2:1, 4-7, emphasis mine).

Is the big picture beginning to come clear? Paul's great prayer of chapter 1 was that we might know the depths of the power of God toward us. That power is like unto that which God exerted in raising Christ from the dead and seating him on the place of authority of the universe without rival. How will we ever know this power? We were trapped spiritually in powerlessness (2:1-3). But God applied the very resurrection of Christ to us and has seated us even now with him in that place of authority. And all of that is ours by virtue of being 'in Christ' (2:6). If Christ has been raised from the dead and we are 'in Christ', then what is our condition? If Christ is at the right hand of God and we are 'in Christ', then where are we positionally? If Christ has all authority in heaven and earth to execute his will and we are 'in Christ', what stands in our way as we go forth to do his will on earth?

> Christ's session is at the right hand of God. His people, therefore, occupy 'with him' the same august position. This honor is not to a chosen few, but is the portion of all those who share the resurrection of the Son of God. It is the birthright of every true believer, of every born again child of God.... The right hand of the throne of God is the center of power of the whole universe, and the exercise of the power of the throne was committed unto the ascended Lord.... The elevation of his people with him to the heavenlies has no other meaning than that they are made sharers, potentially for the present, of the authority which is his. They are made to sit with him; that is, they share his throne. To share a throne means without question to partake of the authority which it represents. Indeed, they have been thus elevated, in the plan of God, for this very purpose, that they may even now exercise, to the extent of their spiritual apprehension, authority over the powers of the air, and over the conditions which those powers have brought about on the earth and are still creating through their ceaseless manipulations of the minds and circumstances of mankind.[1]

Here is the source of our authority – Christ himself. Here is the beauty of being 'in Christ' – his very experiences are our experiences. He died, we died. He rose, we rose. He ascended and is seated at the right hand of God the Father Almighty, we are ascended and seated with him there. He has all authority, he has delegated his authority to his church for the fulfillment of his will and the removal of Satan's resistance to that will.

The key to it all is being 'in Christ'. I have a simple way I try to explain the concept of being 'in Christ' to people. On the shelves in my study sits a small wooden doll that was made in Japan. My wife's parents gave it to her after they traveled to that country some years ago. The hand-painted doll has become an illustration of being 'in Christ' because the doll pulls apart and inside it is hollowed out. In the cavity there rests an identical doll, only smaller. Looking at the doll sitting upon my shelves, one would never guess that there is another doll inside, yet there is. When a person is struggling to apprehend their position 'in Christ' I take hold of the doll and I show them the smaller doll inside and then close it up again. I then ask, 'If I take this doll and put it in my pocket, what happens to the smaller doll inside?' The answer is always the same, 'It goes in your pocket too.' 'Alright,' I say, 'what if I throw this doll out the window? What happens to the smaller doll then?' Again the answer is, 'It goes out the window too.' I repeat the same scenario with different actions taken on the larger doll, always the answer comes back that whatever happens to the larger doll is true of the smaller doll also because it is 'in the larger doll'. 'Then,' I ask, 'if you are "in Christ", where are you right now as far as God is concerned?' The light usually comes on and they recognize they are raised to new life with Christ, they are seated with Christ 'in the heavenly realms, far above all rule, and authority, power and dominion'.

Most believers are surprised when they discover that Christ has delegated his authority to them for the fulfilment of his will. But, before we run off in wild-eyed abandon, it is vital that we understand the *scope* of this authority as well. We are not given his authority carte blanche. Jesus said, 'I have given you authority to trample on snakes and scorpions and to overthrow all the power of the enemy; nothing will harm you' (Luke 10:19).

Jesus' use of snakes and scorpions is taken by most commentators as a figurative reference to various evil spirits. This is clear in that he immediately adds 'and over all the power of the enemy'. Satan is called 'the prince of this world' (John 12:31) and 'the prince of the power of the air' (Eph. 2:2) and seems to have gained a measure of authority over the kingdoms of this world through the fall of man (Luke 4:6). The cross of Christ forever unseated him from any place of legitimate authority he may have usurped. Yet the Scriptures seem to teach that Satan, for all of his wickedness, is rather well organized. Ephesians 6:12 indicates that Satan has a hierarchy of order among his demons and they are organized to seek his will and to endeavour to undo God's will.

The scope of the authority Christ delegates to his people is the spiritual battle with the forces of evil. May we never mistake the bounds of this authority delegated to us. This authority is not over people, rather in the body of Christ we are to 'Submit to one another out of reverence for Christ' (Eph. 5:21). I will never forget how I came to realize the importance of making this distinction. My wife Julie and I have tried to teach our children about the things of the Lord from their earliest days. When the kids were still quite small they understood about 'the enemy' and that he tries to do things that God does not like. Knowing that often children have terrifying experiences at night we taught them that if they are ever scared and feel as if 'the enemy' was trying to scare them they were to say, 'I belong to Jesus, you go away!' We spent a few nights talking about this and praying with them about it, and that was it. We had them practise saying the phrase and reassured them that Jesus was stronger than the enemy and that God promises to 'strengthen and protect you from the evil one' (2 Thess. 3:3). They appeared to grasp the truths (in their own way) and be ready to apply them if need be. My confidence in their level of understanding came crashing down, however, when I came home one evening not long after this and Julie reported to me that Joe did not like the way one of his playmates was behaving toward him and she observed him pointing his finger in her face and sternly announcing, 'I belong to Jesus, you go away!'

The arena for the exercise of Christ's authority is in spiritual warfare against Satan and his demonic spirits, not over one another. 'Our struggle is not against flesh and blood, but against the authorities, against the powers of this dark world and against the spiritual forces of evil in the heavenly realms' (Eph. 6:12). We are called to 'serve one another in love' (Gal. 5:13). But when it comes to dealing with evil spirits we are to confidently assert the will of God and see it advance under his authority.

Our foe is not omnipresent, but he is well organized, carrying out his work through an organization of demonic spirits. Our culture has blinded us to a large extent against perceiving the reality of the spiritual battle we are in. In fact it is quite frightening to many people when they begin to realize the reality of the spiritual beings all around them. I appreciate Dr. Neil T. Anderson's emphasis in this regard. He asks a room full of people to whom he is speaking about the reality of spiritual warfare, 'Do you believe in germs?' Sure, everyone does. 'Do you believe there are germs in this room?' Yes, now that you mention it I'm sure they are all over. 'How many of you have seen any germs in this room this morning?' No one can raise their hand. Germs are a reality, they are all around us and a part of every activity of our day. They are there and we know it, though we do not see them. Frightening isn't it? No, not really. The answer is not to become 'germ focused', worrying constantly about what microscopic warrior will invade your body and do you harm. The answer is to become 'health conscious'. The proper response is to eat well, get plenty of rest, exercise regularly, and practise good personal hygiene. In this way the germs will not get the victory over you.[2]

The same is true when we consider the reality of the evil spirits whom the Bible describes as a regular part of the world in which we live. They are wicked, dark beings. They are intent upon bringing dishonour to Christ and upon destroying his work in and through us. The answer, however, is not to become 'demon-focused'. That would be to hand our enemy the victory without a fight. Rather the Bible calls us to be Christ-focused. Is that not the point of Jesus' warning to the seventy-two disciples who came back from their first ministry assignment amazed over the authority they were able to wield over the demons? 'I have given you authority.... However, do not rejoice that the spirits submit to you, but rejoice that your names are written in heaven' (Luke 10:19, 20).

We are on dangerous ground when we begin to focus too much on the authority Christ has delegated to his children and not on Christ himself. One of Satan's tactics in aiming to rob glory from God is to get us to obsess over the demonic or to become enamoured with authority, anything to keep us from fixing our eyes upon Jesus and rejoicing over the grace he has given us to be his people. 'There are two equal and opposite errors into which our race can fall about the devils. One is to disbelieve in their existence. The other is to believe, and feel an excessive and unhealthy interest in them. They themselves are equally pleased by both errors and hail a materialist or a magician with the same delight.'[3]

Jesus' command is to keep our attention upon our relationship with him. We are to focus on being 'in Christ', to use the Pauline phraseology. We are to keep close to Christ and go about the Master's business.

> God's primary call is for each of us to focus on the ministry of the kingdom: loving, caring, preaching, teaching, praying, etc. However, when demonic powers challenge us in the course of pursuing this ministry, we deal with them on the basis of our authority in Christ and our dependence on him.[4]

How does one keep that focus? 'As you received Christ Jesus as Lord, continue to live in him' (Col. 2:6). How did you receive Christ? In simple trust. In humility. With confidence in his promises. Obeying his will. In holy reverence. That is how we received Christ. That is how we are to continue to focus upon and walk with Christ. That is how we are to experience the victory of Christ, brandishing his authority as the enemy stands in his way, but never becoming demon-focused or absorbed with authority.

'Submit yourselves, then, to God. Resist the devil, and he will flee from you' (Jas. 4:7). That is always God's order – submission to Christ and then, and only then, authority over the enemy. 'Humble yourselves, therefore, under God's mighty hand.... Your enemy the devil prowls around like a roaring lion.... Resist him, standing firm in your faith' (1 Pet. 5:6, 8, 9).

> No one is competent to exercise authority until he has first learned to live under authority.... The effectiveness of the exercise of authority in the name of the Lord Jesus Christ depends on the faith of the believer and the degree to which the believer is living under the authority of God. We cannot expect to be effective in resisting the devil if we are not first in true submission to God.[5]

When we try to exercise the authority of Christ outside of the confines of a life focused upon him and lived submissively under his authority we are on dangerous grounds.

> Some Jews who went around driving out evil spirits tried to invoke the name of the Lord Jesus over those who were demon-possessed. They would say, 'In the name of Jesus, whom Paul preaches, I command you to come out.' Seven sons of Sceva, a Jewish chief priest, were doing this. One day the evil spirit answered them, 'Jesus I know, and I know about Paul, but who are you?' Then the man who had the evil spirit jumped on them and overpowered them all. He gave them such a beating that they ran out of the house naked and bleeding (Acts 19:13-16).

This is all fine and good, but what difference is this to make in the way we live? Our entire quest in considering our aversion to authority is to discover how we might better live within the world God has created. Where are we to exercise this authority? What is it that evil spirits do and where do we encounter their work? Demons do many things, not the least of which is incite fear through their intimidations, foster anxiety, stir up obsessive thoughts and actions, capitalize on besetting sins, and prod us toward pride. Stop for a moment and consider the struggle with fear that many people experience. It is said that the majority of people have had a direct encounter with something spiritual which they do not understand and do not like. 50% of people have been awakened by a 'night terror' at or around three-o'clock in the morning. Typically 50% of people have experienced some kind of a terror attack, accompanied by extreme pressure on the chest or throat, leaving them with the sense that they were unable to respond either physically or spiritually.[6]

How does the child of God deal with these intimidations of the evil one? Prayerfully give thanks to God for the truth of your identity in Christ, submitting yourself to him in joyful obedience. Then confidently resist the evil forces stirring up the fear within, commanding them in the name of Jesus to cease their activities and leave your presence. Return immediately to prayer to God, offering praise and thanksgiving to him for all the good things that are yours in Christ. Then in faith, resting upon Christ, go forward with his will.

How, then, does the exercise of this authority take practical form in the struggles we face? When the dark lion roars with his intimidation how ought we respond? When the deception of the enemy of our souls is foisted upon us how may we dispel it? Allow me to give some practical examples from my own life and ministry which I hope will serve to provide some 'how to' in the exercise of God's authority in Christ.

The Scriptural principle, I believe, is to always stay basic in our relationship to and ministry for Christ (2 Cor. 11:3). This is never more important than when considering standing up to the devil.

I was once asked for counsel from a mature Christian woman who had suddenly begun to experience what, for lack of a better term, the doctors decided to call fainting seizures. She was being used of God in numerous ways and was growing in her faith. There was no precedent in her life for these troublesome episodes. She sought medical answers from several doctors. I encouraged her to continue to do so. She and her husband and I prayed together about the trouble and asked for the Lord's insight. As the weeks went by more and more doctors were baffled by what she was experiencing. Being quite young at the time, I sought the counsel of a more experienced pastor. He rather sheepishly asked, 'Have you ever considered that it might be a spiritual problem?' he quickly added that he did not want me to think that he finds 'a demon under every bush!' I took his counsel and prayed it over. Within a few days, in an entirely unrelated conversation with a family member of the woman, I discovered that there was a history of occult practice and witchcraft in their extended family. At my next meeting with the couple I asked her if she was aware of this background. She knew nothing of it. I suggested the possibility of satanic involvement and urged them to each pray about this possibility. I asked them to watch and see if they might detect any pattern to the fainting seizures.

When we met again they acknowledged that, while they had never considered such a thing, spiritual conflict might be a possible source of the problem. It was discovered that the majority of the fainting seizures occurred at the close of church services or during times of prayer and worship. After simply teaching some basic truths of Scripture and coaching as to how we might pray about this attack, the three of us entered into a time of prayer. Each one of us prayed. The woman prayed to entirely submit herself to Christ, including any areas of her life that unbeknownst to her had been held onto by the evil one. In prayer she took her place in Christ and renounced any footholds that Satan may have held in her life through any family practices or personal involvements in the occult. She again submitted herself specifically and entirely to Christ. I closed in prayer, thanking God for his victory in Christ.

No fireworks flashed. No voices screamed out of the thin air. Nothing strange or seemingly out of the ordinary occurred. But the seizures, which by that time were regularly occurring several times a week, now stopped entirely. As suddenly as they had appeared, they disappeared. For one year there was not a hint of a fainting seizure. Then there were couple of times where they seemed to come back, but again taking her place in Christ she stood her ground in faith and the attacks have disappeared permanently. That took place over ten years ago. Staying basic enabled this woman to step clear of Satan's discouragements and move forward in fulfilling Christ's ministry through her.

On occasion Satan and his demonic forces will be less willing to relinquish ground gained in a person's life. As I have counselled with people and we have gotten nearer to dealing with issues and areas of their lives where Satan has gained a foothold I have seen Satan use a number of tactics to try to sidetrack the process or derail it altogether. On a number of occasions, as I have been leading those I'm counselling through prayer in claiming their place in Christ and standing against the evil one, I have had them tell me they feel nauseated and sick. I simply break in and calmly pray, claiming the victory of Christ and standing against this deceitful tactic of the evil one. Briefly turning from prayer to God through Christ, I directly address Satan and his demons and demand they cease their activity, and then I turn immediately back to God in prayer and praise. I have never failed to see the nausea and sickness immediately subside. On other occasions I have warned people as we begin to pray that Satan may try to scramble their thoughts, creating such confusion in their minds that they can't concentrate or pray intelligibly. Several times those with whom I am counselling have reported that just such confusion is beginning to encroach on their minds. I break in, thank God for the victory we have in Christ, rebuke the evil one, and turn back to God in confident prayer asking for his power to be displayed in the person's mind. Once again, I have never seen God fail to respond to such prayer. Similarly sometimes counselees report that their hearing is suddenly becoming obstructed and they cannot hear what I am saying. A similar response of prayer, rebuke and prayer yields similar results.

Do not get the mistaken notion that such spiritual warfare is mechanical. Some naive people think that such warfare praying is much like a vending machine. You place your coins in the slot, press the button and you get what you want. Some people think that all you do is pray a little prayer, asking for what you want God to do (or the devil not to do), and voila! you get what you asked for. While evil spirits must yield to the authority of Christ, they do not always do so easily or willingly. The key is to stand on truth, pray truth, persevere in truth, and keep holding truth forth. The light of truth dispels the darkness of deception. The authority of the Word of God will bring submission. It is not the power of my prayers verses the power of the devil. It is not the volume or tone of my voice that brings the power of God to bear on a person's life. It is the authority of God bringing the power of God to bear on a defeated enemy through faith-filled servants who hold simply, but tenaciously to the truth of God. The key is to keep standing my ground in Christ.

There is danger, however, in the notion that such encounters must be protracted and drawn out. In fact I urge great caution here. By stubbornly refusing to yield ground won by Christ, the demonic spirits may simply be attempting to wear down the servant of Christ. In their fatigue or discouragement they may be more easily led astray. I once was acquainted with an outstanding young pastor who had planted a church in a needy area and was leading it to dynamic growth. He was a steady, biblical, solid man, husband, father and pastor. One day a woman ventured into their church and gave evidence of coming to faith in Christ. As the weeks unfolded she told her story. She had been a part of an occult group and had been involved in Satan worship. As the pastor and elders counselled her over weeks they began to get worn down. They began to try new things to see if they could not 'win' the prayer battle for her. Before long the pastor and the woman were involved sexually and he announced to the church a vision from God that laid out a map of the future of the world (which was not biblical). He divorced his wife, married the woman and split the church. Though the story is a much longer one than we can describe here, it stands as a warning to stay basic and allow God to do his work through his word as we stay faithful.

One year ago my wife and I spent some time ministering for Christ in West Africa. Since that time our church has sent a team of ten men to that same area in order to minister for Christ. I was not a part of the team, but helped prepare them for the ministry there. During their time in Africa I was awakened in the middle of the night with a start. I immediately sensed an almost overwhelming presence of evil. The last image in my mind as I jolted awake was an almost indescribable face of what can only be characterized as a mutation of demonic and human features. Feeling nearly unable to breathe, I nevertheless began to call on Christ, praising him, appropriating his victory and taking my place in Christ. I commanded the evil presence to leave me. I prayed for our men who at that very hour were active in ministry for Christ in Africa. God granted me to fall asleep again nearly as quickly as I had been awakened.

What to make of this? Simply a mental projection of a worried pastor? Or the attack of Satan's minions because he did not appreciate the ministry for Christ our church was bringing to a region long held by him? I have no doubt it was the latter. I have no doubt that the authority of Christ, taken up by faith expressed through prayer, was victorious in the brief skirmish in the war already won by my Saviour.

These are but a sampling of the many ways in which Satan will seek to intimidate and deceive the child of God. He is as creative in his work as he is wicked. Therefore, we could not possibly enumerate the many tactics he employs as he seeks to rob God of his glory. The particular way in which the evil one seeks to discourage you from walking in God's will may not have been described. Yet it is my hope that these few examples will provide a model for putting into action the truth of the authority of the believer. For when one stands 'in Christ', faithfully and persistently exercising his authority to accomplish his will in his way and in his time, God will grant his power to overcome the intimidations, accusations, deceptions and efforts of Satan. In this way God will be glorified in the particulars of our daily experience and we will find our lives joyfully joined with the eternal purposes of God.

NOTES

1. John A. MacMillan, *The Authority of the Believer* (Harrisburg, Pennsylvania: Christian Publications, Inc., 1980), pp.17-18.

2. Neil T. Anderson, *Resolving Spiritual Conflicts*, video curriculum (La Habra, California: Freedom in Christ Ministries).

3. C. S. Lewis, *The Screwtape Letters* (Charlotte, North Carolina: Commission Press, Inc., 1976), p.17.

Embracing Authority

4. Neil T. Anderson, *The Bondage Breaker* (Eugene, Oregon: Harvest House Publishers, 1990), p.71.

5. Timothy M. Warner, *Spiritual Warfare* (Wheaton, Illinois: Crossway Books, 1991), pp.74-75.

6. Neil T. Anderson, *Resolving Spiritual Conflicts*.

9

The Authority of God and Preaching

Preaching is as integral to Christianity as was the process of weaving to the clothing you now wear. Preaching is not the substance of Christianity – that pre-eminent place belongs to Jesus Christ alone. Nor is preaching the designed end of God's purposes for man – glorifying himself by bringing people into a life-changing encounter with his Son Jesus Christ is that goal. Preaching is the divine-human weaving instrument through which God, utilizing our efforts, brings the person of Jesus Christ and ordinary people into union. Preaching is the God-ordained means through which the living person of Jesus is woven as an integral and inseparable part of the lives of his people. Preaching is God introducing people to Jesus Christ and then his introducing Jesus Christ into every part of their lives.

John Stott affirmed the centrality of preaching to Christ's purposes when he said, 'Preaching is indispensable to Christianity. Without preaching, a necessary part of its authenticity has been lost. For Christianity is, in its very essence, a religion of the Word of God.'[1]

If preaching truly does hold such a central place in the very nature of Christianity, how then does it relate to the authority of God? An issue that is ever before those whose lives are under the call of God to preach his Word is that of authority. What is authority in preaching? How can one detect when one has preached with authority? Does authority have to do with volume? Or is it more determined by the demeanour, facial expression and general countenance of the one delivering the sermon? Or perhaps authority has more to do with the relationship of the speaker to the hearers? Is control over another's life the same as authority? Does any authority the preacher has arise from some subjective experience they claim to have had with God when he 'told' them what to say?

By no means is this issue of authority in preaching a simple topic. Perhaps we are best served by making a distinction between preaching with authority and talking in an authoritarian manner.

Speaking as an authoritarian has more to do with components of the delivery such as volume, demeanour and other elements of non-verbal communication such as facial expression, gestures and body language. Indeed, Albert Mehrabian has shown that nonverbal communication may have a significantly higher impact in what is taken from a message than do even the particular words chosen by the preacher. He suggests that the total feeling of the message is determined as follows: 7% verbal, 38%vocal and 55% facial.[2] So one may be speaking forth a very empathetic, compassionate word about God's love, but be communicating an authoritarian message because of the style of delivery. While we proclaimers of God's Word have been given a message that rings with authority, we have not been called to stand over the people and berate them in an authoritarian manner.

If authority in preaching is not determined primarily by volume, demeanour, facial expression and other elements of nonverbal communication, by what is it determined? How can we identify a message that has authority? Perhaps even the form of that question begins to answer our need. Are we looking for a message that has authority or a messenger that has authority? Do I have any inherent authority within myself as I stand to preach? Or is it a delegated authority? Is any authority I may carry to the pulpit inherent in a position I hold within the church? Or is the authority a delegated one, one I can take no credit for or wield independently? R. Albert Mohler has stated the issue well: 'The authority of the preacher is intrinsically rooted in the authority of the Bible as the church's Book and the unblemished Word of God.... We speak because God has spoken, and because he has given us his Word.'[3]

The only authority any one may legitimately claim is that authority which alone belongs to God. God delegates his authority to us when he hands us his Scriptures and calls us to preach them. To the degree we speak what God has spoken in holy Scripture, to that same degree we speak with authority. Where we speak with cleverness and cuteness we may entertain and coddle, but we do not preach with authority. People go home with bloated bellies and starved spirits where there is no authoritative proclamation of God's word.

Luther underscored this sad kind of preaching which is misled into thinking that being contemporary means something less than keeping one's finger on the text of Scripture.

> This is the way it has gone with preaching.... After the text of the Gospel is read, they take us to fairyland. One preaches from Aristotle and the heathen books, another from the papal decretals. One brings questions about blue ducks, another about hen's milk.... In short, this is the art in which nobody sticks to the text, from which people might have had the Gospel.[4]

Mohler again drives to the point when he says, 'The issue of authority is inescapable. Either the preacher *or* the text will be the operant authority.' And he warns us 'of confusing our own authority with that of the biblical text. We are called, not only to *preach*, but to preach *the Word*'.[5]

We must make one more distinction in this matter of authority and preaching. The preacher's authority arises from the text of Scripture and the proclaimer's fidelity to it, not from a subjective experience they may claim to have had with God. Momentarily I will outline the absolute necessity of having a call from God to preach and the process of submission to God through the personal study of the Bible and the demand for complete dependence upon the Holy Spirit working in and

,h us and our urgent need of prayer before we dare preach s Word. However, at this point, we must distinguish between authority that arises from an experience we have had and the authority of God which lies within the truth of the text of Scripture.

Paul warned the Galatians, 'But even if we or an angel from heaven should preach a gospel other than the one we preached to you, let him be eternally condemned!' (Gal. 1:8). Paul did not discount the spiritual nature of the experience, only the authority of it. Paul, likewise, warned the Corinthians of those who would come preaching another Jesus or another gospel and he warned them against receiving another spirit (2 Cor. 11:4). Did Paul deny that such people had gone through some sort of spiritual experience over which they were quite exercised, even to the point of demanding its authority? No, Paul identified such as a spiritual experience (2 Cor. 11:14), but denied its authority as coming from God.

Experience alone does not constitute authority. 'Feeling' like God wants you to say something is not the same as having authority when you preach. Our only authority is that which is inherently God's and embodied in the text of Scripture.

God's Word is in itself living and active and sharper than any two-edged sword (Heb. 4:12). God's Word is not dependent upon the character or godliness of its proclaimer in order for it to work (Phil. 4:15-18). God's Word always accomplishes what it is sent out to do (Isa. 55:11). We should not, however, assume that the dry reading of Scripture alone by one who is not indwelt by and filled with the Holy Spirit qualifies as biblical preaching. James S. Stewart said that one element of the preacher's authority rests in the fact that he 'must possess the Word – or rather, he must be possessed by it – as a living, personal experience. Why is it that two men, enunciating the very same truths, may differ utterly in results achieved? The one declares the salvation of Christ, and little or nothing happens. The other, using almost the identical words, declares the same salvation, and chords are set vibrating in a hundred hearts. It is in the realm of personal experience that the difference lies.'[6]

Our authority comes from the text of Scripture, but it must be delivered under the empowering of the Holy Spirit to be biblical preaching. So, in one sense, there is experience necessary for authority in preaching – the experience of God the Holy Spirit pulling the preacher through the knot-hole of divine truth in Scripture and then pouring that truth of holy Scripture through the clean vessel of the preacher. Our every experience must be governed by the text of Scripture, and our every proclamation of the text of Scripture must be empowered by the Holy Spirit. When those two elements come together as we step into the pulpit the apostle Peter's words come true: 'Each one should use whatever gift he has received to serve others, faithfully administering God's grace in its various forms. If anyone speaks, he should do it as one speaking the very words of God' (1 Pet. 4:10-11a).

How then can we see the authority of God restored to the preaching of his Word in the churches? There are, in my understanding, several keys to this restoration of divine authority in preaching. First of all must be the return to the biblical understanding of the task of preaching. To do this it would do us well to consider the primary Greek words of the New Testament that inform our understanding of preaching. Though exhaustive word studies are not possible given the narrow focus of the task at hand, we would do well to consider the meaning of words such as *kerusso, euangelizo, parakaleo, martureo, anangello, anaginosko, exegeomai, laleo, dialegomai, phegomai* and their related words groups.

From a survey of these words, however, what may we conclude about the nature of New Testament preaching? While lexical studies alone are not the only basis for drawing final conclusions, a study of the relevant Greek words reveals that preaching, in its nature, is an act endued with authority by God. The preacher is accountable to God for the clear communication of the divine message. As one under authority the proclaimer of God's Word is not free to change the message, but must send it forth accurately. To the degree that the representative of God has accurately communicated the God-given message, the authority of God in preaching should likewise compel the recipients of the message to receive it as it is, the Word of God to them. Preaching is, however, centered not in a person called a 'preacher', but in the dynamic act of God working through the individual to communicate a divine word to mankind. Whatever method or manner in which the preacher delivers the God-given message it should be God and his message that are left as the lingering impression upon the hearer's minds, not an impression of the preacher.

While preaching is accomplished under the authority of God, it should not be seen as a wholly grim and threatening task. The message is an announcement about Jesus Christ and thus is 'good news'. This sense of 'good news' should govern not only the content of the message, but also the manner and demeanour in which it is delivered. Preaching is never to be a detached report of what God has said, but rather the bearing witness of one personally affected by the God he serves and whose personal life has come under the scrutiny of the very message he bears. Preaching is not a mere ethical exhortation that is detached from factual undergirding. Rather, preaching provides substantive factual content about God, his ways, his purposes and his provisions so that the exhortation and call to respond to God rest upon his enabling and not our religious effort.

The second key to restoring authority to the preaching of God's Word is a divine reminder of the message we are called to preach. What is the message entrusted by God to the New Testament preachers? We will take two tracks in answering this question: first, we will examine the book of Acts to discover what was the content of the message they preached; second, we will examine the New Testament and discover the phrases used to describe the message we are sent forth to make known.

The book of Acts records thirteen different occasions in which the gospel was proclaimed (Acts 2:14-40; 3:12-26; 4:8-12; 5:29-32; 7:1-53; 10:34-43; 13:26-41; 14, Paul was interrupted and not allowed to finish in this instance; 17:22-23; 22:1-21; 24:1-17; 26:1-32; 28:17-29). A survey of these accounts of preaching reveals the essentials of the gospel preached by the church in its earliest stage. The essential elements of the gospel as proclaimed by the early church included the Messiah's sufferings, his resurrection, a call for the hearers to repent, the promise of forgiveness, that the message being proclaimed was according to the Scriptures, and that this message is for all peoples.[7] These elements are found in virtually every circumstance in which the early church proclaimed the gospel and the message was recorded. These items were either explicitly declared or implicitly assumed in the proclamation of the gospel.

What do we proclaim? Jesus Christ – God's appointed Saviour who suffered and died for the sins of all people – and that for those who will repent and believe forgiveness is available from God – all of this tied to and proclaimed out of the holy Scriptures.

Having now seen this historical record of the early church, we can examine the statements from the epistles concerning what is the message we are to proclaim. In so doing, we discover the same emphasis arising from the epistles. While an author of Scripture may mention only one aspect of this total message at a particular point, an overview of all that is said about the message of New Testament preaching reveals the same emphasis.

What do the New Testament letters reveal the message of preaching to be? Jesus is that message. 'For I received what I passed on to you as of first importance: that Christ died for our sins according to the Scriptures, that he was buried, that he was raised on the third day according to the Scriptures, and that he appeared to Peter, and then to the Twelve' (1 Cor. 15:3-4).

In Jesus Christ the specifics of his death by crucifixion (1 Cor. 1:23-2:2), his resurrection from the dead (1 Cor. 15:4), and his Lordship (2 Cor. 4:5), the forgiveness of sins and reconciliation to God (2 Cor. 5:18-20) form the core of the message we proclaim. Other various descriptive phrases of the message proclaimed also occur: 'the word of faith' (Rom. 10:8), 'the faith' (Gal. 1:23), 'the gospel' (Gal. 2:2), 'the gospel of God' (1 Thess. 2:9), 'the gospel of Christ' (1 Cor. 9:12), 'the gospel of the glory of Christ' (2 Cor. 4:4), 'the testimony about God' (1 Cor. 2:1), 'the word' (1 Cor. 15:2), 'this mystery' (Eph. 3:9) and 'the cross' (Gal. 5:11). Paul sounded the cry that Jesus and all that God has and will accomplish through him is our only message. There is no other message for the New Testament preacher (Gal. 1:8-9; 2 Cor. 11:4).

The New Testament epistles emphatically declare that all of this proclamation must take place out of and in adherence to the written Word of God. Paul concluded his letter to the Romans by declaring that God 'is able to establish you by my gospel and the proclamation of Jesus Christ ... now revealed and made known through the prophetic writings' (Rom. 16:25-26). All of Paul's preaching was 'according to the Scriptures' (1 Cor. 15:3-4). Peter, quoting the Old Testament prophet Isaiah, said: 'but the word of the Lord stands forever.' And this is the word that was preached to you' (1 Pet. 1:25). Paul reminded Titus that the message he preached was 'promised before the beginning of time, and at his appointed season he brought his word to light through the preaching entrusted to me' (1:2-3). In fact Jesus is seen to be the fulfilment and substance of every promise previously made by God. 'For the Son of God, Jesus Christ, who was preached among you by me and Silas and Timothy, was not "Yes" and "No", but in him it has always been "Yes". For no matter how many promises God has made, they are "Yes" in Christ' (2 Cor. 1:19-20). The ongoing commission of God's appointed proclaimers today is to 'Preach the Word' (2 Tim. 4:2).

It is of note that on several occasions the apostle Paul made reference to 'my gospel' or 'our gospel' (e.g., Rom. 16:25; 2 Tim. 2:8; 1 Thess. 1:5). The gospel could only be spoken of as being Paul's, or anyone else's, in the sense that they had first of all been captured by it personally and compelled by it through divine calling. The gospel is not 'ours' in the sense that we own it or have rights to alter it. We are accountable to God for the purity and preservation of the message he has entrusted to us. However, it is indeed desirable for a preacher of God's Word to be so captivated and compelled by it that it has become, in one sense, 'his' through personal encounter with God.

What then is the message we are sent forth to proclaim? The answer from both the historical record of the early church in Acts and the teaching of the New Testament letters is the same. Ultimately our message is not a 'what', but a 'who'. Jesus Christ is our message – he is God's appointed Saviour who suffered and died for our sins and was then raised from the dead. Those who turn to God's offer of grace in Jesus Christ through repentance and faith find peace with God and the forgiveness of their sins. This message, for the New Testament preacher, must be communicated in such a way that the hearers understand it comes with authority from the written Word of God and is not of the proclaimer's invention.

The third key to restoration of authority to preaching is to remember our calling. The necessity of having a call to preach the Word of God seems to be a fading concept in some circles. When, however, one moves away from some of the prevailing opinions and back to the Bible you discover afresh the necessity of being called by God to preach the Word of God.

One need look no further than the example of the preachers of God we find in Scripture. Jeremiah was convinced of God's call upon his life: 'Before I formed you in the womb I knew you, before you were born I set you apart; I have appointed you as a prophet to the nations' (1:5). If you tried to convince Isaiah the call to speak for God was not necessary, you would have had a fight on your hands: 'Then I heard the voice of the

LORD saying, "Whom shall I send? And who will go for us?" And I said, "Here am I. Send me!"' (Isa. 6:8). Amos had no doubt about God's call: 'But the LORD took me from tending the flock and said to me, "Go, prophesy to my people Israel"' (Amos 7:15).

The New Testament yields a similar sense of divine calling by those who spoke for God. Paul was emphatic about his call to preach. Note how he described himself to the Galatians, 'Paul, an apostle – sent not from men nor by man, but by Jesus Christ and God the Father, who raised him from the dead' (Gal. 1:1). John and Peter similarly knew theirs was a divine calling (Rev. 1:19; Acts 4:20).

It is relatively simple to state the necessity of being called to preach the gospel, it is significantly more difficult to describe what a calling from God is. For Isaiah and Paul being called by God as his spokesmen was a dramatic event, full of earthshaking and life-changing phenomenon (Isa. 6; Acts 9:1-19, 22:3-21, 26:12-18). For individuals such as Amos, John and Peter the circumstances were more simple and less cataclysmic (Amos 7:15; Matt. 4:18-20; Mark 3:13-19).

Indeed, if you ask a dozen preachers to share about their call to ministry you will likely finish with twelve different testimonies. God is incredibly creative and consistently personal in the way he deals with his servants. It would be impossible to state 'the' way in which God calls his spokespersons.

However, having said this, are we left to float alone amid a sea of subjective feelings in trying to ascertain if we are called by God? No. While the circumstances of the encounters wherein we became convinced of God's call are many, there are common elements that seem to be true of each one of our callings.

I would place as the number one element of a call by God to preach his Word a sense of divine compulsion. There must be a 'have to' about our preaching. There come days when we would rather not preach – perhaps because of some internal

162

subjective sense of unworthiness or perhaps because of the weight of the message God has given us to deliver. Martin Luther confessed to such days, saying, 'If I could come down with a good conscience, I would rather be stretched out on a wheel and carry stones than preach one sermon.'[8] Who has not occasionally so felt the weight of the responsibility of preaching God's Word that we could not echo Luther's words?

Yet it is in these very times we must know that we are under divine appointment, lest we prove unfaithful. To use Luther's words again, we know we cannot come down from the pulpit having failed to deliver God's appointed word and still maintain 'a good conscience'. I understand Spurgeon said it before him and others since him, but Lloyd-Jones has described the need well.

> I would say that the only man who is called to preach is the man who cannot do anything else, in the sense that he is not satisfied with anything else. This call to preach is so put upon him, and such pressure comes to bear upon him that he says, 'I can do nothing else, I must preach.'[9]

Was it not this divine compulsion which drove Jeremiah to confess, 'But if I say, "I will not mention him or speak any more in his name," his word is in my heart like a burning fire, shut up in my bones. I am weary of holding it in; indeed, I cannot' (Jer. 20:9). Was it not the sense of divine compulsion which drove Amos to say, 'The lion has roared – who will not fear? The Sovereign LORD has spoken – who can but prophesy?' (Amos 3:8). Paul similarly cried out: 'Woe to me if I do not preach the gospel!' (1 Cor. 9:16).

This seems to have been the testimony of many of the great proclaimers of God's Word in the past. 'I wanted to preach,' said C. H. Spurgeon. R. G. Lee described his call as 'An irresistible urge....' 'Preach! Preach! he seemed to cry in my heart,' was Lee Scarborough's testimony of the encounter with God wherein he became convinced of his call.[10]

A modern day testimony of divine compulsion comes from the pen of Frank Pollard when he shares words written in the early days of his ministry.

> I am a preacher for the same reason that Moby Dick was a whale. I can't help it. It is what I was born to and created for. My only ambition is to be a communicator of God's truths found in his Word. My one goal is to state the great, old truths of the Bible in simple, fresh ways.
>
> My only tools are words, short, simple words born in the love of God. It is as impossible for me to see preaching as dull, tedious work as it is for a bird to dread to fly. I've tried to arouse my interest in many hobbies, but each dulls quickly as the desire to share his good news in new ways constantly claims the passion of my heart. This is God's will for me. It is good![11]

Other elements seem to be consistent in the circumstances of the call of God in different people's lives. There should be a firm conviction concerning the truth and authority of the Word of God (2 Tim. 3:16-17). There should be an understanding of spiritual gifts and how they are distributed in the church and your life (Eph. 4:11-12; 1 Pet. 4:10-11). There should be a powerful infilling of the Holy Spirit for daily life and ministry (Eph. 5:18; 1 Cor. 2:4-5). There should be conviction concerning the necessity of gospel proclamation (Rom. 10:12-17). There should be the affirmation of the church upon your sense of call (Acts 13:1-3). There should be an unwavering conviction that God, and God alone, has the right to call a person to proclaim his Word and where his call is issued, ability to fulfil that call is assured (Jer. 1:4-8). Paul asked, 'Who is equal to such a task?' (2 Cor. 2:16). Paul quickly answered his own question: 'Not that we are competent to claim anything for ourselves, but our competence comes from God' (2 Cor. 3:5).

Donald Hamilton is correct. 'The circumstances of the call are not important. The assurance of the call is. It is this assurance that gives a sense of steadfastness and stick-toitiveness when unjustified criticism comes or failure seems likely.'[12]

The particulars of how God worked out his call on my life may not match the details of how he worked it out in your life, but the fact of his call is something all preachers must share in common. In fact Oswald Chambers may not have overstated the case when he wrote:

> If you can tell where you got the call of God and all about it, I question whether you have ever had a call. The call of God does not come like that; it is much more supernatural. The realization of it may come with a sudden thunderclap or with a gradual dawning, but in whatever way it comes, it comes with the undercurrent of the supernatural, something that cannot be put into words.[13]

We have established that God alone calls a person to the preaching ministry and that he will do it in his own unique way and that the individual must be convinced of this call. To what, however, is the individual called? To a vocation? To a career? To an occupation? No, none of these things forms that to which the preacher is called. The preacher of God's Word is first and foremost called to relationship, a relationship with the living God. The call of God is a call to himself and to the constraints of obeying whatever his will and Word may direct you to do. Much could be said here about the relationship of the preacher to God, but that we will take up in a moment. Let me say here that in our modern world where we hear so much talk of careers, professionalism, vocation and occupation we need to distinguish between these things and the call of God. The words of Ben Patterson are helpful here.

> Our vocation is our calling to serve Christ; our occupations are the jobs we do to earn our way in the world. While it is our calling to press our occupations into the service of our vocation, it is idolatrous to equate the two. Happy is the man or woman whose vocation and occupations come close. But it is no disaster if they do not.
>
> If tomorrow I am fired from my job as pastor ... and am forced

to find employment in the Sonoco station down the street, my vocation would remain intact. I still would be called to preach. Nothing would have changed my call substantially, just the situation in which I obey it.

As Ralph Turnbull points out, I may preach as the paid pastor of a church, but I am not being paid to preach. I am given an allowance so that I can be more free to preach.[14]

The fourth key to seeing the authority of God evidenced in the preaching of his Word is to remember the nature of the work to which he has called us. What exactly is preaching? We have considered the nature of preaching, but have not as yet advanced a definition of preaching. Defining preaching is no easy task because preaching is a living, divine action and as such can never be adequately contained or constrained by the mere words of man. However, we might define preaching as the proclamation of the Word of God, in reliance upon the Holy Spirit, so that the original intent of the biblical author is made clear and the enduring relevance of the Scriptures are made plain for the contemporary listener. But this definition of necessity leaves much assumed and unstated. The aforementioned definition of preaching may include within its circle what has been commonly known as topical, textual and expository preaching.

We must go further than this simple definition. I agree with Douglas M. White when he says, 'Again, it is our firm and studied conviction that, in the light of the fact that preaching is primary, the style or method known as *expository* preaching is paramount.'[15] Again we must define what we mean by expository preaching. I define expository preaching as that form of proclamation which, in reliance upon the Holy Spirit, arises from and is delivered through a study of the grammatical, syntactical, literary, historical, contextual, theological and cultural elements of a given biblical text and seeks to convey the abiding and authoritative principles that are inherent in that text and were primary in the original author's intention in such a way that the enduring relevance of the Scriptures are made plain for the contemporary listener.

This would be seen as distinct from other common methods of preaching. Topical preaching would be different in that its goal is not the understanding and communication of one particular biblical text and thus may not as directly seek one biblical author's original truth intention. As a synthesis of various passages by various authors, topical preaching may see its authority in proclamation shift from the biblical text to the preacher's way of connecting the various passages.

Textual preaching, as it is sometimes understood, does focus on one particular passage, but it is usually limited to one or two verses. Without careful study and work the verse or verses may end up being lifted from the flow of the book in which they are found and disconnected from the contextual elements that should aid in informing that text.

Expository preaching places a premium upon the need to study basic thought units of Scripture and the fact that these units are understood only when studied in their contextual framework. Stuart Briscoe's warning is more than appropriate.

> How we're tempted to bend the Word to fit our words! It is a most devious temptation: to preach selectively, to avoid a lot of subjects, to slide by passages we don't want to talk about, to manipulate Scripture to say what I would have inspired it to say had I been the Holy Spirit.[16]

It should be noted that topical and textual preaching need not be unfaithful to the original intent of the biblical authors. In fact some contemporary issues that need to be addressed will probably be best handled by a topical message (i.e. various life issues such as abortion, euthanasia, doctor assisted suicides, etc.). Therefore we should not berate topical or textual preaching as unbiblical, but recognize that it may provide a valid and helpful method of studying the Scriptures. However, having said this, I must state that it is my conviction that expository preaching should be the regular and steady diet served up to God's people in the local church. This accomplishes the systematic teaching of all the truths of the Scripture and models a valid method of study for our people. Topical and textual sermons may supplement this steady diet of expository preaching and thus give broad and well-rounded nourishment from the Word of God.

This understanding of what preaching, and in particular what expository preaching, is, therefore, must of necessity affect every aspect of the work of preaching.

There is a process to preaching. The preparation process cannot be bypassed. As the preacher is preparing the message, God is preparing the messenger. The preacher must work in the text of God's Word and God must work the text into the preacher. Preaching is work; preparing to preach is work. It has been said that preaching is the closest thing a person will ever experience to the labour of childbirth without actually delivering a child. Paul told Timothy,

> Until I come, give attention to the public reading of Scripture, to exhortation and teaching.... Take pains with these things; be absorbed in them, so that your progress may be evident to all. Pay close attention to yourself and to your teaching; persevere in these things (1 Tim. 4:13, 15-16, NASB).

Indeed, Paul again exhorted Timothy in his last correspondence with him, 'Be diligent to present yourself approved to God as a workman who does not need to be ashamed, handling accurately the word of truth' (2 Tim. 2:15, NASB).

A multitude of good things will call the pastor away from the sacred duty to study diligently the Word of God and prepare a spiritual feast for God's people to be nourished on when they gather. The faithful proclaimer of God's Word must be disciplined to study and must be immersed in the Word of God as God prepares him to proclaim his Word. John MacArthur has stated the need better than I can:

> Fling him into his office. Tear the office sign from the door. Nail on the sign, 'STUDY.' Take him off the mailing list. Lock him up

with his books and his typewriter and his Bible. Slam him down on his knees before texts and broken hearts, and the flick of lives in the superficial flock and before a Holy God. Force him to be the one man in our surfeited communities who knows about God. Throw him into the ring to box with God all the night through. And let him come out only when he's bruised and beaten into being a blessing....

When at long last he dares assay the pulpit, ask him if he has a word from God. If he does not, then dismiss him. Tell him you can read the morning paper and digest the television commentaries, and think through the day's superficial problems, and manage the communities' weary drives, and bless the sordid baked potatoes and green beans better than he can.

Command him not to come back until he's read and reread, written and rewritten, until he can stand up worn and forlorn and say, 'Thus saith the Lord.' Break him across the board of his ill-gotten popularity, smack him hard with his own prestige, corner him with questions about God, cover him with demands for celestial wisdom and give him no escape until he's back against the wall of the Word. Sit down before and listen to the only word he has left: God's Word.[17]

The study of the Word of God must take place at the greatest depth possible for the individual pastor. If the original languages are known, or can be learned, the study of the text should include this aspect of study. The busy pastor need not do all the work in the languages himself, many tools are available to aid him in mining the meaning of the text from the original languages. The elements of grammar, syntax and word meanings add much to the understanding of the text. The study of the Word must include carefully investigating the context of the passage to be preached. The context, properly understood, unlocks and informs us as to the meaning intended by the author of Scripture. The preacher must also dig out the larger context of where the text falls within the flow of God's redemptive activity. To whom was it written? What particularly was happening in the lives of those being addressed that warranted this word from God? What cultural elements from the original author's and recipient's settings help inform the text? The student of Scripture must include the literary makeup of the text in their study. What genre of literature does it represent? Is this text poetic, parabolic, narrative, apocalyptic, prophetic or epistolary in nature? The theology of the whole of Scripture must also inform the text to be preached. What has progressive revelation unveiled of God's plan to this point? What other texts parallel or inform this one?

Our study should analyze the text by taking it apart piece by piece, but then it must synthesize by putting it back together piece by piece with a greater understanding of the whole because we have comprehended the parts.

We must also recognize, however, that behind the study process being exacted by the preacher, there is another process being worked out by God the Holy Spirit. While the preacher is taking the text apart word by word, phrase by phrase, sentence by sentence, God is taking the preacher apart, studying the components of his character, scrutinizing his thoughts, judging his tongue, assaying his motives, examining his family life, inspecting his ministry faithfulness. The proclaimer must first come under the floodlight of the truth he intends to proclaim to others. Then while the proclaimer of the Word begins to synthesize and put the pieces of the text back together, God the Spirit works to build his preacher.

Preaching is a process, a process of the preacher submitting time and again to the breaking work of the Holy Spirit through the holy Scriptures. We submit to that process by keeping ourselves diligent in the study so we can experience the dynamic of the Holy Spirit in the pulpit. Perhaps it is this to which Bruce Thielmann spoke when he said: 'The pulpit calls those anointed to it as the sea calls its sailors; and like the sea, it batters and bruises, and does not rest... To preach, to really preach, is to die naked a little at a time and to know each time that you must do it again.'[18]

Preaching is a process of being broken: that happens in the

study, but it also happens as the work of the study follows us through every avenue of our life and work. However, for the one called to preach, the process of being broken by God is well worth the hardship because of the outcome.

> For we do not preach ourselves but Christ Jesus as Lord, and ourselves as your bond-servants for Jesus' sake. For God, who said, 'Light shall shine out of darkness,' is the One who has shone in our hearts to give the light of the knowledge of the glory of God in the face of Christ.
>
> But we have this treasure in earthen vessels, that the surpassing greatness of the power may be of God and not from ourselves; we are afflicted in every way, but not crushed; perplexed, but not despairing; persecuted, but not forsaken; struck down, but not destroyed; always carrying about in the body the dying of Jesus, that the life of Jesus also may be manifested in our body.
>
> For we who live are constantly being delivered over to death for Jesus' sake, that the life of Jesus may be manifested in our mortal flesh. So death works in us, but life in you (2 Cor. 4:5-12, NASB).

In the final analysis William Quayle was correct when he wrote, 'Preaching is the art of making a sermon and delivering it? Why, no, that is not preaching. Preaching is the art of making a preacher and delivering *that.*'[19]

For this reason we must underscore the absolute necessity of the work of the Holy Spirit in every phase of sermon development. From the calling to preach to the closing of the sermon the Holy Spirit is and must be active. From the moment the preacher-to-be is convicted of sin, righteousness and judgement and wooed to faith in Jesus Christ the Holy Spirit's work is essential.

When the call of God to preach is brought home to the heart, the Holy Spirit is active. Through the training and preparation process for preaching, the Holy Spirit must exert his presence and power. When the gifts for ministry are bestowed, it is at the sovereign will of the Holy Spirit that they are given. When a preaching calendar is prepared, the

Holy Spirit communicates the Father's mind to the preparing preacher. When the individual texts are studied, the Holy Spirit must illumine the heart and mind of the preacher to understand the Word. The Holy Spirit must bring the truth of those texts to roost in the preacher's heart and life, pressing home the applications for them, long before the message of these truths can be presented to others. When the message is crafted it is under the tutelage of the Holy Spirit. When the preacher finally steps to the pulpit, the Holy Spirit must be actively present or only the dry crust of parsed verbs and cute stories will be the meal for God's people that day.

Little wonder that E. M. Bounds said that 'Preaching is not the performance of an hour. It is the outflow of a life.' Bounds continued, declaring that

> It takes twenty years to make a sermon, because it takes twenty years to make the man. The true sermon is a thing of life. The sermon grows because the man grows. The sermon is forceful because the man is forceful. The sermon is holy because the man is holy. The sermon is full of divine unction because the man is full of divine unction.[20]

All of that can only be true because of the convicting, regenerating, sealing, sanctifying, gifting, calling, illuminating, instructing and empowering presence of the Holy Spirit. We preachers are absolutely dependent upon God showing up every week as we place ourselves before his Word in our studies. We are shut up to that which God will deliver to us and through us. Apart from him, we can do nothing.

How then can we experience the authority of God in the pulpits of our churches? It begins with a biblical understanding of the task of preaching, advances as we remember the message we are commissioned to preach, grows as we return to our calling to preach, deepens as we give ourselves fully to the nature of the work of preaching, and comes to a climax as we participate in the divine process of preaching. Through these elements we position ourselves to receive the oil of God's Holy Spirit poured upon us in a mighty anointing to preach the Word of God with authority.

Without this anointing our pulpits may be filled with orthodox theology, adorned with clever outlines and illustrations, cajoled with humour, and styled with attempts at relevance, but there will be no authority from God. What then can we conclude concerning this work of preaching? It is hard, it is impossible – apart from the work of God the Holy Spirit.

> A sermon may be constructed after the best models; it may conform to all the rules of homiletics; the text may be suitable and fruitful; the plan may be faultless; the execution may discover genius and judgment; there may be accurate analysis and strong reasoning; proof and motive; solidarity and beauty; logic and passion; argument direct and indirect; perspicuity, purity, correctness, propriety, precision; description, antithesis, metaphor, allegory, comparison; motives from goodness, motives from happiness, motives from self-love; appeals to the sense of the beautiful, the sense of right, to the affections, the passions, the emotions; – a sermon may be all this, and yet that very sermon, even though it fell from the lips of a prince of pulpit oratory, were as powerless in the renewal of a soul as in raising the dead, if unaccompanied by the omnipotent energy of the Holy Ghost.[21]

NOTES

1. John R. W. Stott, *Between Two Worlds* (Grand Rapids, Michigan: William B. Eerdmans Publishing Company, 1982), p.15.

2. Myron R. Chartier, *Preaching as Communication: An Interpersonal Perspective* (Nashville: Abingdon, 1981), p.83.

3. Michael Duduit, ed., *Handbook on Contemporary Preaching* (Nashville: Broadman, 1992), p.15.

4. Henry Grady Davis, *Design For Preaching* (Philadelphia: Fortress Press, 1958), p.91.

5. Duduit, p.15.

6. James S. Stewart, *Heralds of God* (London: Hodder and Stoughton, 1946) reprint, Grand Rapids, Michigan: Baker Book House, 1972, p.217.

7. William J. Larkin, Acts in Historical, Theological, and Missiological Perspective (Columbia, South Carolina: Columbia Biblical Seminary, 1985).

8. Duduit, p.15.

9. D. Martyn Lloyd-Jones, *Preaching and Preachers* (Grand Rapids, Michigan: Zondervan Publishing House, 1971), p. 105.

10. Duduit, p.138.

11. Ibid., pp.137-138.

12. Donald L. Hamilton, *Homiletical Handbook* (Nashville: Broadman Publishers, 1992), p.17.

13. Oswald Chambers, *My Utmost For his Highest* (New York: Dodd, Mead, and Company, Inc., 1935), p.273.

14. Ben Patterson, 'Is Ministry a Career?', *Leadership Journal* (Carol Stream, Illinois: Christianity Today, Inc., summer 1990), p.55.

15. Douglas M. White, *The Excellence of Exposition* (Neptune, New Jersey: Loizeaux Brothers, 1977), p.16.

16. Bill Hybels, Stuart Brisco, and Haddon W. Robinson, *Mastering Contemporary Preaching* (Portland: Multnomah Press, 1989), p.142.

17. John MacArthur, 'The Highest Calling', (Panorama City, California: Word of Grace Ministries, 1992), Cassette GC 80-73.

18. Kent and Barbara Hughes, *Liberating Ministry From the Success Syndrom* (Wheaton, Illinois: Tyndal House Publishers, 1987), p.183.

19. William Quayle, *The Pastor-Preacher* (Grand Rapids, Michigan: Baker Book House, 1979), p.27.

20. E. M. Bounds, *Power Through Prayer*, (Grand Rapids, Michigan: Baker Book House, 1972), p.8.

21. Henry C. Fish, *Handbook on Revivals* (Boston: James H. Earle, 1874), quoted in Lloyd M. Perry, *Biblical Preaching For Today's World* (Chicago: Moody Press, 1973) pp.201-202.

10

The Authority of God and
the Great Commission

The pews were filled. The people had all assembled. The music was seeking to soothe impatient minds that had begun receiving signals from painful seats. The pastor and other church leaders nervously checked their watches. 'Where is he?' The service was beginning and the elderly, visiting preacher was nowhere to be found. A young woman was dispatched by the edgy leaders to rush to the home where he was staying and see what the delay was about. The expectant people fidgeted in suit coats worn but once a week and dresses saved for Sunday.

Soon the girl returned ... without the preacher. 'I did not want to disturb him. He was talking to somebody,' she explained. One among the leaders spoke for all, 'That is rather strange, because everybody is here. Go back and tell him that it is after time and that he *must* come.' The girl raced once more to the home where the aged preacher was staying. Again she returned alone. 'He *is* talking to somebody,' she insisted. 'How do you know that?,' the leaders demanded. She answered, 'I heard him saying to this person who is with him, "I will not go and preach to those people if You will not come with me."' Suddenly understanding the reason for the delay, the pastors replied, 'Oh, it is all right. We had better wait.'

Dr. Martyn Lloyd-Jones told this story about an old Welsh preacher and concluded: 'The old preacher knew that there was little purpose in his going to preach unless he knew of a certainty that the Holy Ghost was going with him and giving him authority and power. He was wise enough, and had sufficient spiritual discernment, to refuse to preach until he knew that he had his authority, and that the Holy Ghost was going with him and would speak through him.'[1]

If we know the authority and presence of the Lord Jesus goes with us we will undertake anything. If, even for a moment, we are unconvinced of his authority with us, even the prospect of standing still will terrorize us. This is not some spiritual phobia, but is the doing of the Lord Jesus himself. He is the one who said, 'All authority in heaven and on earth has been given to me. Therefore go ... And surely I am with you always, even to the very end of the age' (Matt. 28:18-20). Knowledge of the presence and authority of Jesus with us emboldens us against any foe, heartens us in the face of any odds, and inspires us to weather any discouragement.

It is of the utmost importance that we understand what this authority of Jesus is conferred for. When Jesus promises to go with us to the farthest horizon of time, what is it he expects we will be doing along the way? It is wise to carefully answer this question, for Jesus does not write blank checks. Seven sons of Sceva would stand and testify to the folly of trying to wield Jesus' authority independently (Acts 19:13-16). The aged Welsh preacher would rather have taken on a church full of disappointed, disgruntled people than to venture forth without the knowledge of Jesus' blessing upon his ministry.

What has Jesus given his church the authority to do? The simple answer is that he has granted us his authority to fulfil the Great Commission. Yet it is needful to stop and ask some questions: What is the Great Commission? Is there an 'authorized' way of accomplishing it? Or does the end justify any means?

Most startling is Jesus' majestic statement: 'All authority in heaven and on earth has been given to me' (v.18). Sandwiched between Jesus' baptism at the hands of John with the subsequent descent of the Holy Spirit upon him and the inauguration of his earthly ministry, there were the agonizing temptations of the wilderness. 'Again, the devil took him to a very high mountain and showed him all the kingdoms of the world and their splendor. "All this I will give you," he said, "if you will bow down and worship me"' (Matt. 4:8-9). Satan offered Jesus authority without sacrifice. Jesus rejected this cross-less authority, choosing rather to embrace the Father's appointed path of humble service, selfless sacrifice, agonizing suffering and finally the total giving of self in death. Now, having finished the Father's work, he has received in fullest measure the authority over the universe.

Let's not rush by this most amazing declaration of Jesus too quickly. Is the Jesus preached today the One possessing all authority in heaven and earth? 'If we could but stand back and just look at the New Testament and the whole Bible with fresh eyes, I believe we would be rather amazed at the fact that the really big claim which is made in the whole of the New Testament is for the supreme authority of the Lord Jesus Christ.'[2]

What do we make of this statement, 'All authority in heaven and earth *has been given* to me' (emphasis mine)? Did not the Lord Jesus possess divine authority simply by virtue of his nature as God? Yes, most certainly. Let's be clear, Jesus has always possessed full deity. The Son is both co-eternal and co-equal with the Father and Spirit. Jesus, as the second member of the Trinity, shares fully in the divine essence. Yet, for the purposes of redemption he submitted himself to the Father and came to procure the salvation the Father decreed. In this self-imposed limitation Jesus confessed, 'My Father is always at his work to this very day, and I too, am working.... I tell you the truth, the Son can do nothing by himself; he can do only what he sees his Father doing, because whatever the Father does the Son also does. For the Father loves the Son and shows him all he does' (John 5:17, 19-20). 'I do nothing on my own but speak just what the Father has taught me' (John 8:28). 'By myself I can do nothing; I judge only as I hear, and my judgement is just, for I seek not to please myself but him who sent me' (John 5:30). Again Jesus said, 'I have brought you glory on earth by completing the work you gave me to do' (John 17:4).

Jesus clearly exercised authority during his earthly ministry before his resurrection. He declared that he had authority to forgive sins and that he would one day judge all men. Jesus demonstrated his authority over demonic spirits, disease, nature, and even death. Yet never had he made such a lofty claim as this one in Matthew 28:18-20, the claim to possess all authority in every sphere. It seems that the Lord Jesus in his earthly, pre-resurrection ministry operated within the self-imposed limits of dependence upon the Father's will and the Spirit's empowering. While possessing the essence, full rights and prerogatives of deity, in his redemptive mission he chose to subordinate himself and the exercise of his divine prerogatives to the Father. Yet, having died and risen again, what Jesus had always rightfully possessed as a full member of the Trinity is now his, not by virtue of divine nature only, but also by virtue of redemptive reward. The lofty ancient hymn of Philippians 2 describes it best:

> Who, being in very nature God,
> did not consider equality with God something to be grasped,
> but made himself nothing,
> taking the very nature of a servant,
> being made in human likeness.
> And being found in appearance as a man,
> he humbled himself and became obedient to death –
> even death on a cross!
> Therefore God exalted him to the highest place
> and gave to him the name that is above every name,
> that at the name of Jesus every knee should bow,
> in heaven and on earth and under the earth,
> and every tongue confess that Jesus Christ is Lord,
> to the glory of God the Father.

This is mystery deep! Paul knows that understanding of such truth will happen only by the Spirit's enabling (Eph. 1:18). Indeed he prayed that the Ephesians might understand the power that was exerted in raising Jesus from the dead because 'he raised him from the dead and seated him at his right hand in the heavenly realms, far above all rule and authority, power and dominion, and every title that can be given, not only in the present age but also in the one to come. And God placed all things under his feet and appointed him to be head over all things for the church' (Eph. 1:20-22).

It now appears as if Jesus announces something like, 'Before this, according to the redemptive plan, I have been wholly submissive to the Father and have lived my earthly life in dependence upon the Spirit. But now, having secured redemption and having defeated every foe, the Father has handed over to me the final stages of the program of redemption. The Father has placed in my hands what was once mine by divine prerogative, but is now mine also by redemptive right: *all authority* to bring to a close the redemptive work of God!'

Notice that this authority is 'in heaven and on earth'. Jesus possesses all-encompassing authority. Jesus has all authority in heaven.

> The kingly authority of Jesus embraces heaven, all that lives and has its being there, angels and archangels, powers, principalities, might, dominion, thrones, and the saints in glory.
>
> This authority is exercised also over the evil spirit world, whose prince is conquered and despoiled, and whose hosts lie in abject submission beneath Jesus' feet. All the powers of heaven are in his hand to do his bidding without question or pause.[3]

Satan and his hellish hordes of demons seek to thwart the believer and hinder him from living to the glory of God. Wherever a child of God is concerned for the glory of God, the hosts of hell are at attention and working overtime. Yet Jesus here assures his own that, while not ignoring all their intimidations, accusations and deceptions, Satan and his henchmen are completely under his authority.

Likewise the authority of Jesus extends to every part of the earth. The powers of nature, indeed the very nations themselves are the possession of Jesus. The Father said 'You are my Son; today I have become your Father. Ask of me, and I will make the nations your inheritance, the ends of the earth your possession' (Ps. 2:7-8). What Satan offered Jesus by way of convenience, the Father has bestowed upon him as reward for his sacrifice of himself.

Jesus possesses all authority in heaven above and earth below. In the outworking of our lives there is not always such a neat dichotomy between the interplay of the powers of heaven and the affairs of God on earth. Yet wherever they come into conflict Jesus wins.

The authority of Jesus over heaven and earth is eloquently testified to in *Against the Tide*, the biography of Watchman Nee. One holiday season Watchman Nee and five other believers planned to visit a remote island off the coast of China where the gospel had never been received. At the last moment a newly converted Christian by the name of Li Kuo-ching decided to venture along. The party of seven made its way to the island and found rough accommodations with a person on the island willing to take them in.

The next day they began their preaching, but met with no response. The first few days the people seemed to be distracted by all of the activities related to the Chinese new year celebration. After preaching vigorously for nine days and still not finding a hearing the young Li Kuo-ching became impatient. 'What's wrong?' he cried out to the people. 'Why won't you believe?' The locals testified of their totally reliable god Ta-Wang (Great King). His annual festival, revealed through divination, was set for the 11th of the month. The Christians were told that for the preceding 286 years Ta-Wang had produced sunshine and cloudless skies for the day of his celebration. 'Then I promise you our God, who is the true God, will make it rain on the 11th,' demanded the zealous Li Kuo-ching! The crowd latched on to the challenge to their god. 'Say no more. If there is rain on the 11th, then your Jesus is indeed God. We will be ready to hear him.'

Watchman was not present when the events unfolded. But when word reached him he was horrified. The glory of the Lord was at stake and Li Kuo-ching seemed to have hastily committed him to a demonstration of authority he might not be willing to bestow. The seven bewildered Christians returned to their lodging and began seeking God, ready to hear his chastisement for their impetuous act.

Then there seemed to come the thought: 'Where is the God of Elijah?' There came also a deep assurance that there would indeed be rain on the 11th of the month. For the first time in 286 years it would rain on Ta-Wang's parade. God's assurance to them was so complete that it not only dispelled their doubt but sent them out to announce the challenge in every corner.

Later that evening the man housing them described Ta-wang as a local deity who truly guarded the people, protecting them from disease, pestilence and barrenness. There was complete confidence that a god so powerful would not be overthrown on his day of celebration. On top of this he reminded the vigilant believers that if Ta-wang failed, which he would not do, at least the fishermen could be relied upon to forecast the weather rightly several days in advance.

The next dawn rang in the morning of the 11th. Watchman Nee was awakened by a ray of brilliant sunlight streaking through an attic window and into his eyes. A bit panicked, he arose and then dropped to his knees praying, 'Lord, please send us that rain!' Once again came the assurance, 'Where is the God of Elijah?'

The seven believers made their way down the stairs and to the host's waiting breakfast of rice. As they bowed their heads they all took notice that the skies were cloudless. In quiet prayer they reminded the Lord of his promise ... before the Amen could be said they heard a few patters of raindrops upon the tile roof. By the time they were well into their bowls of rice there was a steady shower. Being served a second bowl of rice, they prayed and asked God to send even more rain. Before the end of the second bowls of rice could be consumed

181

the rain was torrential. When they finished breakfast they looked out to find the street deep in water and the three steps leading to the home submerged.

A few of the younger residents of the village were heard to shout over the rain, 'There is God; there is no more Ta-wang! The rain has kept him in!' But the more faithful of Ta-wang's followers did not concede his defeat so quickly. They attempted to proceed with his parade despite the flooding. They took the idol into the streets in procession as usual, but slipping and falling the idol crashed to the ground breaking pieces off in the process.

Quickly the idol was taken indoors and divination revealed, conveniently enough, 'There has been a mistake! We have the wrong day! The festival is to be on the 14th with the procession at six in the evening.' The believers in Christ assured the villagers that once again God, the true God, would send rain.

The afternoon of the 11th the weather cleared and they went forth to preach. Thirty people turned to Jesus Christ in faith over the next three days. The 14th brought a similar downpour and the power of Ta-wang was broken over that island and its people.[4]

All authority in heaven and on earth belongs to Jesus Christ. He sits unrivalled at the right hand of the Father. Jesus possesses the sovereign right to exercise the power of God for the purposes of God that he might bring about the full manifestation of the glory of God. What, then, we may ask, are the purposes of God for which this authority has been conveyed to Jesus? Jesus himself answered the question in his next breath: 'Therefore go and make disciples of all nations, baptizing them in the name of the Father and of the Son and of the Holy Spirit, and teaching them to obey everything I have commanded you' (Matt. 28:19-20a).

There are many commands to be found among the records of Jesus' teaching. All of them vital, none to be rejected. Yet the one command of God most clearly connected with the exercise of the authority of God in Christ is this – the command to make disciples of all nations. To this he has most assuredly pleged his authority. To this undertaking he has guaranteed the full backing of heaven. The accomplishment of this end is backed up by Jesus with all the resources of the divine omnipotence.

What, then, is the heart of the Great Commission? When we observe the words of this Great Commission of Jesus, there appear to be four key ingredients: go, make disciples, baptizing, teaching. While all four contribute to the understanding of Jesus' commission, only 'make disciples' is an imperative. 'Go', 'baptizing' and 'teaching' are all participles supporting the one command to make disciples. First consider the heart of the Commission, then we will return to consider the supporting participles. What does it mean to make disciples? What is a disciple?

Jesus' words 'make disciples' is one of only twenty-five times the verbal form of the root word is found in the New Testament. Surprisingly of these twenty-five occurrences only six of them appear in the Gospels – the very place one would expect to find the greater concentration. In contrast we discover that the noun form is found 264 times, all of them in the Gospels. The New Testament tells us a great deal about what a disciple is, but is not nearly so descriptive when it portrays the kind of learning a disciple does in action. Lets contemplate Matthew's understanding of what it meant to be a disciple of Jesus.

A disciple is one who attaches himself to another in order to learn from him. Matthew portrays a disciple as one who has willingly and unconditionally yielded his entire life to Jesus Christ as the most significant relationship one has (Matt. 10:37) and recognizes that this state of yieldedness is incumbent upon him for the entire span of his life (Matt. 10:24ff.). To be a disciple means to be utterly constrained to Jesus Christ and his directives (Matt. 12:46-50). Following Jesus as a disciple requires renunciation (Matt. 23:7ff.), humility (Matt. 18:19), poverty (Matt. 19:23ff) and a readiness to suffer anything rather than turn back from following him (Matt. 10:17ff).[5]

Our commission as followers of Jesus is to make others to be what we already are: people completely yielded to Jesus Christ in a commitment that will endure any hardship or pay any cost simply to be able to continue in our relationship of learning with him. In a world where independence and individualism have been made desirous virtues and where rights are to be demanded, what more humanly impossible task could Jesus have given us? What strategy did Jesus leave us that might give us a reasonable expectation that this commission might be fulfilled among the people we know? Let's return to those three participles to find the answer.

Remember that there is one command ('make disciples'), but it is attended by three participles ('go', 'baptizing' and 'teaching'). These three participles in some way support or further clarify the command. Commentators have been notoriously divided as to their function. Many say that the three participles describe 'how' the command is to be fulfilled. Others say that, though they are participial in form, we must recognize that they too carry an imperatival quality (in other words that they too are commands, not just strategy). It would seem to me that they give us both a means or strategy for fulfilling the seemingly impossible task of making such completely sold out followers of Christ as well as urging us forward in the implementation of that strategy.

How are we going to see selfish, independent, self-confident people become fully devoted followers of Jesus Christ? One prong of the strategy is summed up in the word 'go'. As others have often said, it has the literal sense of 'as you are going, make disciples'. Jesus would seem to be telling us that the fulfilment of this commission is not going to take place primarily in the classroom, sanctuary, or lecture hall. The fulfilment of this commission will come as we are moving out in a Great Commission lifestyle. Jesus' words appear to be something like this: 'Go! Be what you are – fully devoted disciples. As you take this discipleship to the streets others will hear your call to follow Jesus and see what it means to take up that call.' The Great Commission is a lifestyle, not an occasional or periodic activity. The Great Commission must become the passion of our lives, our constant orientation point and our governing authority for the way we go about living life. The boardroom is every bit as much a part of the Great Commission as is the Sunday school room.

The strategy of 'go' also shows us that a disciple is not made in a moment. Discipleship is not an event, but a process. As we 'go' we are seeking the event of bringing people to decisive faith in Jesus Christ, yet we are aiming not at that event alone, but the process of their continuing to follow after Jesus. 'He appointed twelve ... that they might be with him' (Mark 3:14). If we are to make disciples as Jesus made disciples then we must adopt a Great Commission lifestyle, going out to live our lives on purpose among the people God has placed in our sphere of influence and exposing our life in Christ to them and inviting them to share in it. It is as if Jesus is saying to us, 'I give you all authority to change the way you live life. I give you all authority to narrow the field of what you do. I give you authority to live a particular, peculiar lifestyle – one pointed toward the one aim of making others fully committed followers of Me.'

Jesus added a second prong to the threefold strategy of the Great Commission – 'baptizing'. In the book of Acts we hear of many people being baptized. It was their initial, public declaration of identification with Jesus Christ and his followers. Having gone out to live this intentional kind of life and having secured the event of a person's conversion to faith in Jesus Christ, now you have authority to call them to go public with this new life.

In his book *Deliver Us From Evil* Ravi Zacharias has captivatingly chronicled the process of privatization that has swept over our culture. Dr. Zacharias has said, 'Privatization may be defined as the socially required and legally enforced separation of our private lives and our public personas; in effect, privatization mandates that issues of ultimate meaning be relegated to our private spheres.'[6] As we go forth to live this Great Commission lifestyle we will see God use us to call others to the decisive event of trusting Christ as their Saviour. Having been warmed by the notion of freedom from sin and escape from judgement some will, in keeping with the times, enthusiastically embrace Christ on a personal, private level. Yet when called to 'go public' with their commitment some will baulk. Yet Jesus' commission is clear. He says to us, 'You have all my authority to fly in the face of popular opinion about the place of personal, ethical, religious views and call people to stand up and be counted as mine!' This will be for many their first step of counting the cost of discipleship.

Having gone forth to live this Great Commission lifestyle, having been used of God to win people to faith in Christ and having likewise seen them stand up and be counted for Christ before their family, friends, neighbors, co-workers and new Christian family ... there is one last prong to Jesus' strategy for disciple making: 'Teaching them to obey all that I have commanded you.' With their profession of faith in Christ secure, we must not pause to notch our evangelistic belt, for the commission is not complete. We are commissioned by Jesus to employ all his authority in thoroughly intertwining every word he said with every fiber of their being. Ongoing teaching with a view to total, absolute obedience to Jesus Christ is the final prong to Jesus' threefold strategy for the fulfilment of the Great Commission.

We do well to recognize that this is teaching with a view not to a full head, but an obedient heart. Existing as a part of the information age, many Christians have assumed that 'knowledge is power'. We can parse the Greek verbs and diagram the Bible's sentences, but far too often we are impotent to overcome the temptations that the world system puts around us, our sinful nature within us, or the devil and his hordes below us throw down in our path. The apostle Paul described the kind of teaching Jesus had in mind: 'But the goal of our instruction is love from a pure heart and a good conscience and a sincere faith' (1 Tim. 1:5). Love is the goal of teaching; love toward God and love toward others. Has that not been the divine desire from the beginning? Are those not the two divisions of the decalogue? Did Jesus not answer the inquisitive teacher of the law, '"Love the Lord your God with all your heart and with all your soul and with all your mind." This is the first and greatest commandment. And the second is like it: "Love your neighbor as yourself." All the Law and the Prophets hang on these two commandments' (Matt. 22:37-39)?

A disciple of Jesus Christ is one who loves him with his whole being. To bring this love relationship to its fullest, Jesus issues his authority to teach his words. This kind of ongoing teaching brings the Great Commission to rest on a strategy of three stable legs. This kind of teaching is designed to see the learner walk away from the instruction and live differently because they have been caused to look outward toward others with pure motives ('love from a pure heart'), inward in self-judgement ('love from ... a good conscience'), and upward without pretence or hidden agendas ('love from ... a sincere faith').

Look again at Jesus' strategy for bringing people into a totally yielded walk with him: It begins with us living a Great Commission lifestyle that issues forth in others being brought to the event of conversion and open identification with Jesus and his people. The commission then leads to a lifelong love relationship with Christ that grows ever deeper as the truth of his Word is discovered and deployed practically in their everyday lives. 'For this,' declares Jesus, 'you have all My authority! Pursue this and nothing on earth or in hell will ever overcome you!' Life cannot offer us guarantees, but this one guarantee has the backing of the omnipotence and sovereign authority of God himself.

Jesus is telling us, 'For this narrow, counter-culture lifestyle, for this business of calling people to identify with me, for this lifelong task of bringing them into a fully heart-felt obedience based upon my Word – for this I confer upon you my authority!' But please understand, it is not as though he hands his authority to us as a thing, rather he pledges to us his very self. 'All authority in heaven and on earth has been given to me ... surely I am with you always, to the very end of the age.' The promise of his presence is our guarantee of success. The uninterrupted immediacy of his company is our authority in this world. Christ is ultimate authority, with his presence as we do his will we brandish his authority.

The key to authority in the Great Commission is not a new evangelistic trick nor a novel program bound in a colourful album. We will move forward in the fulfilment of the Great Commission when we yield to the Person of Christ and allow his life to be our life. It is 'Christ, who is your life' (Col. 3:4) who is your authority. As we live this Christ-life he who possesses all authority will accomplish his Great Commission work through our ordinary lives with extraordinary authority and power. In this Christ-life we can, along with the aged Welsh preacher, arise and go forth with confidence and authority to join Christ in what he is doing to bring God's redemptive program to completion. What a high privilege! As we allow Christ to live his life and accomplish the Father's work through us we are given the authority to usher in his very return (Matt. 24:14; 2 Pet. 3:12)!

Regarding the tenure of Christ's authoritative presence with us in his work, Jesus closed with this promise: 'And surely I will be with you always, to the very end of the age' (Matt. 28:20). More literally it might be translated 'all the days until the completion of the age'. Jesus promises us that not a day will pass until the ages end that he will not be with us in this pursuit of making disciples. Not a sunrise or sunset will transpire in which we will not have his authoritative presence to deal with that day's obstacles and opposition to his work.

Let us never forget: when we adopt Christ's mission and appropriate his presence, we advance with his authority.

NOTES

1. D. Martyn Lloyd-Jones, *Authority* (Carlisle, Pennsylvania: The Banner of Truth Trust, 1984), p.88.

2. Ibid., p.15.

3. R. C. H. Lenski, *The Interpretation of St. Matthew's Gospel* (Minneapolis, Minnesota: Augsburg Publishing House, 1943), p.1171.

4. Angus Kinnear, *Against the Tide* (Fort Washington, Pennsylvania: Christian Literature Crusade, 1978), pp.91-96.

5. Dietrich Muller, *Dictionary of New Testament Theology*, Colin Brown, ed. (Grand Rapids, Michigan: Zondervan Publishing House, 1971), 1:488-489.

6. Ravi Zacharias, *Deliver Us From Evil* (Dallas: Word Publishing, 1996), p.105.

11

The Authority of God and Servanthood

'Promise me something!' Smiles and reassuring nods of the head accompany the words, but somewhere inside you're suspicious. Promise you what? What do I have that you want? Why do you want it? What do you know about it that I don't?

Jesus was asked essentially that very question by two of his most intimate disciples. 'Then James and John, the sons of Zebedee, came to him. "Teacher," they said, "we want you to do for us whatever we ask"' (Mark 10:35). Read it again, this time put the emphasis on the word *whatever*. Their question was designed to gain them, without the necessity of explicitly asking for it, the places of supreme authority when Jesus came into his Kingdom.

If the strategy of James and John was a bit suspect, from a human standpoint their timing was perfect, or so it seemed. They posed their question to Jesus while they 'were on their way up to Jerusalem' (10:32). Jesus had an appointment with the cross. He had been explicit about the suffering that awaited him on at least two previous occasions (8:31; 9:31) and he was about to expound upon it again (10:32-34). Clearly, however, 'they did not understand what he meant and were afraid to ask him about it' (9:32). What James and John did see was that Jesus was determined to make it to Jerusalem and was keeping a pace along the way that astonished even the disciples (10:32).

James and John must have reasoned something like this: 'This is it! The Kingdom is coming soon! Look how determined Jesus is to make it to his royal city. Victory awaits us just up the slopes of Zion!' In their zeal, James and John probably also concluded, 'These other bozos don't get it yet, but if we word it right I bet we can get Jesus to give us a blank check to be cashed in when we get there!'

What we see in these two disciples looks a great deal like a reflection in the mirror. Clearly, to desire authority is human. The natural human quest is to be well guarded, positioned strategically, leveraged well. All of us avoid the vulnerability of being under authority as the knee-jerk reaction of the fallen nature we possess. We want to be in authority, we want nothing to do with being under authority. To desire authority is human. But like James and John, we may be a bit sheepish about saying it plainly.

I wonder what a tape recording of my last five days of private prayer would sound like? Better (or is it worse?) yet, I wonder what a tape of what I meant by what I prayed over the last five days would sound like? Jesus knows our hearts and he calls us to be specific in our requests. 'What do you want me to do for you?' (10:36), is his response to our vague petitions. It is in the specifics that we are exposed. 'Let one of us sit at your right and the other at your left in your glory' (10:37).

Ah, there it is ... the raw sewage of selfishness, undiluted egotism. It is a rather ugly thing when exposed for what it is. Notice the response of the other ten disciples, 'When the ten heard about this, they became indignant with James and John' (10:41). Do we dare conclude the word 'righteous' should be placed before 'indignation' here? Hardly. Theirs was a pharisaical concoction made of one part anger over having been beaten to the punch and one part hypocrisy in attempting to cover it with a facade of spirituality. The ten were no better than the two ... or than us.

This grasping after authority, position and leverage can be unearthed at virtually every level of human relationships. It finds a seed-bed whenever two people join company ('Let's see, how can I get her to ...?'). This clutching at self-protection at other's expense happens among committees ('If we hurry and get our event on the calendar that will mean they won't be able to!'). Whole churches practise it ('Come worship with us! We are the caring church in town!').

Perhaps it is in our striving to bring about social change that we look most like James and John. In a visit to Chicago, Randal Terry called Christians to become 'intolerant zealots' when it comes to 'baby killers, sodomites, condom-pushers, and that pluralism nonsense'. Terry described their Congresswoman as 'a snake, witch, and evil woman'. He issued a call to the Christians of the city, saying: 'I want you to let a wave of hatred wash over you. Yes, hate is good.... We have a biblical duty, we are called by God to conquer this country.'[1]

Even Ralph Reed, formerly of the Christian Coalition and normally rather circumspect in his speech, spoke of the power-tactics conservative Christians must adopt if we are to see change in the social order. Reed said, 'It's better to move quietly, with stealth, under the cover of night.... I want to be invisible. I do guerrilla warfare. I paint my face and travel by night. You don't know it until you're in a body bag. You don't know until election night.'[2]

Philip Yancey wrote, 'It grieves me that mailings from conservative religious groups read, in tone, much like mailings from the ACLU and People for the American Way. Both sides appeal to hysteria, warn of rabid conspiracies, and engage in character assassination of their enemies. In short, both exude the spirit of ungrace.'[3]

James and John show us that to desire authority is human. That is all it is. Sometimes grasping after authority 'works', but only in achieving human dreams, only in getting what you want, only in perpetuating the world as it is, albeit under a religious banner.

To desire to wield authority is human, but to display humility is divine. If your goal is to get ahead then by all means employ the means of authority. If your desire is to put your foot on your competitor's throat, then by all means position yourself well, cut them off, beat them to the punch.

It works, if your goal is only human. If, however, you are interested in doing something more than perpetuating the status quo, if you want to exalt Christ, if you want to walk with God, if you want to see something supernatural happen, then your strategy will have to change.

Jesus outlined a three-pronged strategy for the triumph of the Kingdom of God in our sphere of influence. Jesus showed us how to maximize the glory of God through our lives. This three-pronged strategy enables us to achieve the purposes of God in the midst of a world clamouring after authority.

The first prong of Jesus' strategy is this: glory proceeds from suffering. When our kinsmen according to our moral nature, James and John, asked for positions of authority, Jesus told them 'You don't know what you are asking.' We think we see the big picture, but God has built into the warp and woof of the universe the principle that true glory proceeds out of suffering. William Culbertson once said, 'Keep praying, and be thankful that God's answers are wiser than your prayers!'

Jesus went on to explain to his two disciples why they did not understand the implications of their request. Jesus answered with a question, 'Can you drink the cup I drink or be baptized with the baptism I am baptized with?' In the Old Testament the cup was a metaphor used to speak of trouble, suffering and judgement against sin (Ps. 75:7-8; Is. 51:17-23; Jer. 25:15-28). Similarly the imagery of baptism had already been used by Jesus to refer to his coming passion (Luke 12:50). He was to be submerged in the agony of God's wrath against our sin. Jesus was on his way to Jerusalem under a schedule that would place him at the cross. Could James and John drink that cup?

'"We can," they answered.' Clearly, when the glitter and gleam of the throne has caught our eye, we don't see the price that must be paid to sit in a place of authority. 'Jesus said to them, "You will drink the cup I drink and be baptized with the baptism I am baptized with, but to sit at my right or left is

194

not for me to grant. These places belong to those for whom they have been prepared.'"

In Christ's Kingdom, glory proceeds out of suffering. Interestingly enough the only other time in the Gospel of Mark that the words right and left are used in tandem is in chapter fifteen when two other characters were found to be on Jesus' right and left. This time, however, it was not in glory, but as they hung upon their own crosses on either side of Jesus.[4] Jesus exercised his authority and began his reign from a cross. To think that we can attain glory and exercise authority without following him with crosses upon our shoulders is to seriously miss the call of discipleship.

I think of Joseph Damien, a missionary of the nineteenth century who gave his service to victims of leprosy on the island of Molokai, Hawaii. Joseph had endeared himself to his flock through much personal sacrifice. He embraced those no one else would touch. But when counting the cost of following his Lord there, not even Joseph understood the price he would be called to pay. Just before leaving to go lead his believers in worship one morning, Joseph was pouring freshly boiled water into a cup. Some of the scalding water poured over the edge and landed upon his bare foot. Nothing. No sensation. No pain. It took a moment for the realization of what had happened to sink in. Seized by panic over what this might mean, Joseph did a most remarkable thing – he poured more boiling water over the bare foot. Once again there was no sensation.

That morning as Joseph Damien strode to the pulpit to deliver the message he had prepared, no one in the congregation much noticed the tears streaming down his cheeks. Scarcely anyone noticed that Joseph began his message differently that morning. Normally he began each message with, 'My fellow believers.' However, this morning his first words were, 'My fellow lepers.'[5]

No suffering – no glory. Philip Yancey in characteristic eloquence illustrates this Kingdom principle for us.

During the volcanic eruption of Mt. St. Helens, intense heat melted away the soil, leaving bare rock coated with a thick mantle of ash. Naturalists of the Forest Service wondered how much time must pass before any living thing could grow there. Then one day a park employee stumbled across a lush patch of wildflowers, ferns, and grasses rooted tenaciously to a strip of the desolation. It took a few seconds for him to notice an eerie fact: this patch of vegetation formed the shape of an elk. Plants had sprouted from the organic material that lay where an elk had been buried by ash.[6]

The Kingdom of God takes root where people are willing to serve to the point of suffering. Out of their sacrifices spring the blossoms of God's purposes. Glory proceeds out of suffering.

The second prong of Jesus' strategy is this: greatness proceeds from servanthood. Mark tells us: Jesus called them together and said, 'You know that those who are regarded as rulers of the Gentiles lord it over them, and their high officials exercise authority over them. Not so with you. Instead, whoever wants to become great among you must be your servant' (10:42-43). Warren and David Wiersbe have well said, 'We abdicate neither our position nor our authority when we serve others. Instead, we prove that it's safe for the Lord and his people to give us that position and authority.'[7]

The story of Nina Cameron and her daughter Natalie are etched permanently in my memory banks, retrieved each time God reminds me that greatness comes through servanthood. Nina regularly took five-year-old Natalie to visit a local nursing home. There they encountered one woman so surly and offensive that no one else wanted anything to do with her. Yet the Lord placed a burden of love upon Nina's heart. She began trying to reach out to the woman and be her friend. Every effort was rebuffed. The harder Nina tried to show the love of Christ, the more the woman withdrew in self-protection. But Nina persevered. One day she asked the woman, 'Isn't there anything you like?' The woman made only partial eye contact and mumbled, 'I like butterscotch candy and I like to draw.'

Nina tried to investigate a bit further about the woman's interest in drawing. She glared at Natalie and gruffly said, 'Well if you could get her to sit still, I'd draw her picture.' Soon Natalie was perched upon her bed and the aged hands began to move with skill as she traced upon notebook paper a beautiful likeness of the little girl. Something seemed to spring to life within her as the woman drew. When the picture was done the woman withdrew again into her cantankerous disposition. Nina stocked the woman well with paper and pencils, but her failing eyesight prohibited her from completing the projects she started.

The woman's calculated rejection of all of Nina's efforts at expressing kindness continued. She didn't even care for Nina's name. For some strange reason she determined to call her Luke. Each time Nina came she was greeted with, 'Luke, did you bring me some butterscotch candy?' The rest of each visit was regularly spent complaining about every conceivable part of her life. Once Nina offered to bring her Bible and read to her, but the woman said, 'Luke, I don't like that religious stuff, and I don't want to hear anything about it again.'

Nina and Natalie continued in their quest to break through the walls of the woman's heart with the battering ram of God's love. During one of her visits Nina discovered that the woman had developed cancer. She spent long days in the hospital. After returning to the nursing home, Nina continued to visit her, one day inquiring about her family. 'I have a son, but I haven't seen him in over six years,' the woman said.

Nina says, 'As I left the nursing home that day, there was a burden and a heaviness of heart that I cannot explain. It was as though Jesus himself was in the car with me.' Arriving home she called directory assistance for New York and gave the name of the woman's son. Dialing the number, she did not know what to expect. When a man's voice answered the phone Nina introduced herself and told how she had been visiting his mother in the nursing home. There was a long, dead silence. Nina prayed silently for the Holy Spirit to break through the pain of the past. In that moment the man began to weep. He said, 'Lady, I don't know who you are, but I love my mother.'

Nina discovered that he did not have the money to visit his mother. She paid for his plane ticket. At one point he said through tears, 'Why are you doing this, lady?' 'Because I am a Christian and in the Bible Jesus said, "When you have helped the least of these, you have done it unto me."' With the many years between them, Nina was not sure what to expect when the son walked into his mother's room. But when they fell into one another's arms and wept, Nina slipped out knowing she had done the right thing. Once again the woman had drawn a beautiful picture, this time the sketch pad was Nina's memory and the pencil was the joy in the woman's eyes.

Son and mother spent several days together. He sat beside her bed, rubbing lotion on her dry skin, drawing pictures she had taught him to draw as a child, talking and most importantly just being together. As Nina took him back to the airport he said, 'There are not words in the English language to express how I feel.' Nina shared about how Christ had changed her life and how it had only been the love of Jesus flowing through her that had enabled her to continue to love his mother.

When Nina returned to the nursing home she found the woman with a contented face full of peace. This time the cold rebuffs were gone. The woman took Nina's hand and said, 'Luke, I love you.' Then she said, 'I want you to bring that Bible when you come back and read it to me.'

The woman died before Nina's next visit. But she had died having tasted of the love and grace of God. She died knowing that God loved her.[8] In God's Kingdom greatness proceeds out of servanthood. I suggest to you that Nina Cameron and her spiritual tribe will be seated nearest Jesus when it is all said and done.

The Jesus-strategy for advancing the purposes of God stands upon three legs. The third prong of Jesus' strategy is this: first place comes from taking last place. Jesus told his disciples that 'whoever wants to be first must be slave of all' (Mark 10:44). Like Joseph Damine and Nina Cameron, Christine Haggai has made the principles of Christ's strategy stand up, walk among us and take us by the shoulders, and shake us into the realization of how God intends to advance his purposes. Listen to the words of Christine's husband, John Edmund Haggai, as he recounts their story.

The Lord graciously blessed us with a precious son. He was paralyzed and able to sit in his wheelchair only with the assistance of full-length body braces. One of the nation's most respected gynecologists and obstetricians brought him into the world. Tragically, this man – overcome by grief – sought to find the answer in a bourbon bottle rather than in a blessed Bible.

Due to the doctor's intoxication at the time of delivery, he inexcusably bungled his responsibility. Several of the baby's bones were broken. His leg was pulled out at the growth center. Needless abuse – resulting in hemorrhaging of the brain – was inflicted upon the little fellow. (Let me pause long enough to say that this is no indictment upon doctors. I thank God for doctors. This man was a tragic exception. He was banned from practice in some hospitals, and, as mentioned previously, he committed suicide.)

During the first year of the little lad's life, eight doctors said he could not possibly survive. For the first two years of his life my wife had to feed him every three hours with a Brecht feeder. It took a half hour to prepare for the feeding and it took another half hour to cleanup and put him back to bed. Not once during that time did she ever get out of the house for any diversion whatsoever. Never did she get more than two hours sleep at one time.

My wife, formerly Christine Barker of Bristol, Virginia, had once been acclaimed by some of the nation's leading musicians as one of the outstanding contemporary female vocalists in America. From the time she was thirteen she had been popular as a singer – and constantly in the public eye. Hers was the experience of receiving and rejecting some fancy offers with even fancier incomes to marry an aspiring Baptist pastor with no church to pastor!

Then, after five years of marriage, tragedy struck! The whole episode was so unnecessary. Eight of the nation's leading doctors said that our son could not survive. From a life of public service she was now marooned within the walls of our home. Her beautiful voice no longer enraptured public audiences with the story of Jesus, but was now silenced, or at best, muted to the subdued humming of lullabies.

Had it not been for her spiritual maturity whereby she laid hold of the resources of God and lived one day at a time, this heart-rending experience would long since have caused an emotional breakdown.

John Edmund, Jr., our little son, lived more than twenty years. We rejoice that he committed his heart and life to Jesus Christ and gave evidence of a genuine concern for the things of the Lord. I attribute his commitment to Jesus Christ and his wonderful disposition to the sparkling radiance of an emotionally mature, Christ-centered mother who has mastered the discipline of living one day at a time.[9]

How does God advance his purposes? In God's Kingdom glory proceeds from suffering, greatness from servanthood and first place is arrived at by taking last place. For all the power of the living, breathing illustrations of these principles by people like Joseph, Nina and Christine, they would all agree with Mark when he says that Jesus best modelled this three pronged strategy he calls us to. 'For even the Son of Man did not come to be served, but to serve, and to give his life as a ransom for many' (Mark 10:45).

To serve another in true humility is to wield the most irresistible authority known among men. To desire authority is human; to display humility is divine. The one breeds power plays, posturing, and a warfare mentality. It is the push that invites a shove, that evokes a trip, that elicits a punch, that ends with our hands around another's throat. What begins as an intention to ascend to a place of authority ends as a descent into the self-destruction of selfishness.

To desire authority is indeed human, but to display humility is divine. Humility operates on the fulcrum of grace. Servanthood dismantels the armourment of relational warfare. It disables the memory banks of bitterness. It relaxes the fist. It opens the heart. Grasping after authority is the human way, the world's way, the devil's way to the top. Humble service is Jesus' way to the throne. The only steps by which we may ascend to the throne and reign with Christ begin by going downward. The ascent to a place of God-given authority is achieved only through self-imposed descent into service, humility and suffering.

Perhaps no more powerful modern illustration of the clash between the ways of man and the strategies of Christ can be found than what took place at the 1994 Presidential Prayer Breakfast in Washington, D.C.

In a city that pulses with power, authority, position and leverage there walked a diminutive four foot six inch dynamo of servanthood. She spoke of how selfish America has grown. Exhibit one, she said, is abortion. The slaughter of our innocent is evidence enough of our basic bent toward self. With the powers-that-be in attendance and the most powerful people in the world in her hand, she spoke words of truth. Words that had to be listened to, even by those who disagreed with her. Those in attendance were compelled to listen because she brought with her an eighty-four year old trail of selfless service to the world's most unwanted people – the despised people from the gutters of Calcutta, India.

That day, by everyone's accounting, Mother Teresa, weak in body, frail in stature, fragile of voice, nevertheless thundered with authority. It was the moral and spiritual authority of one who had walked in the steps of her Master. 'Their great men exercise authority over them. But it is not so with you....'

Asked later to comment on Mother Teresa's words – words that obviously tread upon President Clinton's personal views – he said simply, 'It is very hard to argue against a life lived so well.'[10]

Glory from suffering. Greatness from service. First place from taking last place. A strange way to build a kingdom? Perhaps in the world's eyes. But where we walk in the Master's steps we wield the Master's authority. And the world must stand up and take notice.

NOTES

1. Philip Yancey, *What's So Amazing About Grace?* (Grand Rapids, Michigan: Zondervan Publishing House, 1997), p.210.

2. Ibid.

3. Ibid., p.221.

4. David E. Garland, *The NIV Application Commentary: Mark* (Grand Rapids, Michigan: Zondervan Publishing House, 1996), p.411.

5. Ravi Zacharias, *Deliver Us From Evil* (Dallas, Texas: Word Publishing, 1996), p.186.

6. Yancey, p.231.

7. Warren W. and David W. Wiersbe, *10 Power Principles for Christian Service* (Grand Rapids, Michigan, Baker Book House, 1997), p.66.

8. Dennis Rainey, 'Family Life Ministries Newsletter' (November 1, 1992).

9. John Edmund Haggai, *How to Win Over Worry* (New York: Walker and Company, 1987), pp.154-156.

10. Zacharias, p.201.

12

The Authority of God and the Close of History

A quick look at the morning paper is all the evidence needed to convince most folks the world is a mess. We're confused by it all. Where are we headed? Is anyone in control? If not, toward what are we careering? How fast? How abrupt will be the stop at the other end of this wild ride we call human history? Such questions may not rise to the level of our conscious thoughts on a daily basis, but they are not far beneath the surface of our frantic efforts just to deal with 'today'. The confusion and disgust with things as they are has led many to cynicism. Take for example the book handed me by a friend a while back. It is entitled simply, *Life Stinks*. Listen to the introduction.

> It's sad but true that fate stays in the background most of our lives, showing up only to hand us the fuzzy end of the lollipop. The overwhelming weight of evidence proves that life stinks: If there's a fifty-fifty chance of the toast falling on the floor buttered side down, why does it do so 99 percent of the time? There is no rhyme, no reason, and absolutely no justice. It seems there's only one certainty in life – it's unfair. The diner sitting next to you at the lunch counter will always be served a sandwich that looks fresher and bigger and is surely tastier than yours, especially when both orders are identical. Tollbooth lines, barking dogs, income taxes, bad hair days, Barney, Biosphere II – does anyone need more proof of life's pungent aroma?
>
> Only blind optimism could doubt the facts, and, as everyone knows, optimism is the belief that everything is beautiful (including what is ugly) and that everything wrong is actually right. In real life, the light at the end of the tunnel is usually an oncoming train. How else can you explain the fact that just as you are on your way to the most important job interview of your life a pigeon will

inevitably leave a comfortable perch on a statue and aim directly at you? The optimist proclaims that we live in the best of all possible worlds, and the pessimist fears that this is true. The realist understands that life's odor is often unpleasant.

The truth of the matter is that we're all bound by Murphy's Law, which states that anything that can go wrong, will go wrong, especially when you least expect it. Just when you think nothing can go awry, Dame Fortune is there quietly slipping lead into her boxing gloves. One minute life is a bowl of cherries, the next you're knocked out cold. But don't take it personally. Take a look at the frustrated and grim faces around you and you'll realize that *life stinks* – not just yours, everyone's.[1]

The fact that life stinks, at least part of the time, is bad enough. Most of us can handle a bad day now and then. It is when those days begin to string together that we get worried. The emerging pattern of misfortune casts a grey gloom over our whole outlook. For the most part we can swallow hard and accept a bad day, but deep down we may begin to ask ourselves if it is going to stay this way? Stuart and Doris Flexner, in their book *The Pessimist's Guide to History*, have answered that question with a strong affirmative.

A pessimist habitually sees and anticipates the worst, believes we live in a world of gloom and doom, and that there is more pain and evil in the world than goodness and happiness. At the risk of championing this defeatist attitude, I have to admit that most major events in the history of the world tend to support this viewpoint.[2]

One of the popular arguments against acknowledging the authority of God is the state of the world. How can a loving God allow all of this? Where was God when my little brother died? Why doesn't God clean up this mess? In short, we demand justice! Life appears to be quite unfair. Children die while molesters live. How can this be? Simple, ordinary folks starve to death while their ruthless dictator prospers upon his throne. Why doesn't God put an end to it? Increasingly it seems the corrupt collect the power while the virtuous vanish from the public scene. Where is God in all of this? We want justice to fall from heaven!

We are not unlike the disciples of our Lord. At least five times in Mark's record of the life of Jesus his followers called him to account for his response to their problems (Mark 4:38; 5:31; 6:37; 8:4, 32). 'Teacher, don't you care?' (4:38) was the cry of their heart when they were overwhelmed.

Job, even in his great patience, was finally provoked into questioning God. I have counted 110 questions that Job asked God. Suffering will do that to a person. Some people will tell you that questions are wrong when directed toward God. I don't agree. It is fine, even commendable, to ask God questions; Noah, Abraham, Moses, David, all the greats of the faith, did. We must, however, be careful to distinguish between asking God a question and questioning God. Suffering often greases the slope that divides the two. For Job, the suffering he endured eventually moved him out of asking God questions and into questioning God. Job questioned God's justice. How did God respond? He didn't. He doesn't have to. One of the great lessons we need to learn is that it is fine to go ahead and ask God our questions – he wants our openness and honesty – but to realize that he does not have to answer us. God owes us nothing. However, finally, graciously, God did respond to Job. What did he say? God turned the tables on Job and now he asked his servant seventy questions of his own. Why? Because Job needed to see what we need to see ... ultimately it isn't answers to our questions that we need, but to learn to ask the right questions. Warren Weirsbe suggests that God's seventy questions can be shuffled together into three more basic queries: Can you explain My creation (38:1-38)? Can you oversee My creation (38:39-39:30)? Can you subdue My creation (40:6-41:34)? In essence Job was questioning God's knowledge, power and justice.[3]

The fact that we share a contemptuous inquiry with some greats of the faith does not relieve either our curiosity or our culpability. What should we make of God's apparent silence?

What conclusion ought we to draw with regard to what appears to be Divine inactivity? Is there slumber in heaven while the faithful suffer? Not at all. In fact God has revealed to us that he is at work. Our trouble is that even if he completely disclosed his plans to us we would not be able to fully understand them (Hab. 1:5). God has not penciled in the details of all that will be, but he has given us the broad strokes of the final expression of his authority that will close human history as we know it. What we can see is sufficient to dispel all doubt and invite us to the peaceful trust afforded true worshippers.

The apostle Paul describes something of the mystery of the ultimate triumph of the authority of God in 1 Corinthians 15:24-28.

> Then the end will come, when he hands over the kingdom to God the Father after he has destroyed all dominion, authority and power. For he must reign until he has put all his enemies under his feet. The last enemy to be destroyed is death. For he 'has put everything under his feet'. Now when it says that 'everything' has been put under him, it is clear that this does not include God himself, who put everything under Christ. When he has done this, then the Son himself will be made subject to him who put everything under him, so that God may be all in all.

History is linear, not cyclical. We are not caught in an unending experience of living through the past's reruns. We are headed somewhere. There is coming a time, in 'the end', when the authority invested in Christ by the Father will have been brought to its end goal. The kingdom of God will win. Justice will be served. All opposition will be put down. All 'dominion, authority and power' will have been destroyed. Christ will be Victor! Finally and forever all that displeases and dishonours God will be under his feet! Having won the battle he was sent for, Jesus will hand the kingdom over to the Father once again. He then 'will be made subject to him who put everything under him'. Think of it! Mystery of mysteries! How can the co-eternal, co-equal Son eternally subject himself to the Father with whom he shares all the prerogatives and essence of Deity? 'The passage is a summary of mysteries which our present knowledge does not enable us to explain, and which our present faculties, perhaps, do not enable us to understand.'[4] Though our minds cannot fully comprehend it, this implies no inferiority of the Son to the Father either in his person, nature, or dignity. It simply means that even the Son, without surrendering his deity or dignity, is willing to subject himself eternally to the Father so that the authority of the triune God might be forever a wonder the new creation can't take its eyes off.

When these unsearchable events have played themselves out, then 'God will be all in all'. The end goal of all the universe – from creation to consummation – will have been achieved! God will have been seen to be the source from which all things flow and the goal toward which all things progress. His glory will be manifested in its fulness! This has been the target from time immemorial. 'As I live, all the earth will be filled with the glory of the LORD' (Num. 14:21). This was God's repeated promise and prophecy throughout the Old Testament. This was the affirmed pledge of God himself as his people stood upon the threshold of the promised land and refused to be part of his grand progress toward this display of his own glory (Num. 14:21). Such was the desire of Solomon at the height of the Old Testament kingdom's glory. 'Praise be to his glorious name forever; may the whole earth be filled with his glory' (Ps. 72:19). This was the heart cry of the prophets of the Lord as they beheld the corruption of God's people and the crumbling of the Old Testament kingdom during its final centuries. 'For the earth will be filled with the knowledge of the glory of the LORD, as the waters cover the sea' (Hab. 2:14). '... the earth will be full of the knowledge of the LORD as the waters cover the sea' (Isa. 11:9). 'The LORD will be king over the whole earth. On that day there will be one LORD, and his name the only name' (Zech. 14:9). Now, through Christ, this is the blessed hope of every child of God. 'But our citizenship is in heaven. And we eagerly await a Savior from there, the Lord Jesus Christ, who, by the power that enables him to bring everything under his control, will transform our lowly bodies so that they will be like his glorious body' (Phil. 2:20-21). One day a rider on a white horse will split the skies and bring in a radiant flood of God's glory throughout all creation (Rev. 19:11-21). Finally and forever all opposition to God will be put down (Rev. 20).

There is a time coming when the sound of countless millions of knees will be heard as they hit the dust in humble submission to Christ (Phil. 2:10-11). Some will bow willingly, having practised for that day in untold times of personal worship during their sojourn upon earth. They will bend low in joy as they pass into a life of bliss forever in the presence of their Saviour and Lord. Others will have their unyielding knees bent low under the awesome weight of the unveiled glory of God in Christ. Having never acknowledged Christ in this life, they will be compelled to bend low in worship before him then. Theirs will be a parting admission of his rightful place even as they pass out of his presence forever into eternal torment. Either way, all will bow.

Likewise we are told every tongue will utter the confession 'He is Lord!' To some it will be the sweet, final echoes of their heart's song, having been sung through difficult days as they trod this life. Their song will become an eternal song of worship. Others will find the words forced over lips that have cursed and slandered his name all their lives. Even as their teeth begin to gnash and their eyes begin to weep, without any hope of comfort throughout eternity, they will finally utter those words: 'He is Lord!' All alike, however, will verbally acknowledge what will have become the most obvious conclusion of all creation – Jesus is Lord!

Then, with all humanity recognizing him for who he is, Jesus will take his place in glad submission to the Father and the brilliant light of his glorious Person will become the perpetual lamp of the New Jerusalem. Then will the goal of the triune God be achieved and he will be all in all.

The beauty of the apostle's words are only enhanced when we stand back just enough to behold them in the setting of their context. This multi-faceted jewel of what will be is found in a setting of what has already been – the resurrection of Jesus from the dead. Gordon Fee says, 'Paul's point is that in raising Christ from the dead God has set in motion a chain of events that must culminate in the final destruction of death and thus of God's being once again, as in eternity past, "all in all".'[5]

Why doesn't God do something? How can I understand the authority of God when the world is in the state it is in? God has done something! He has entered our world and lived completely and perfectly as a man. He died in our place, bearing the punishment of our sin. Three days later he was vindicated by being raised from the dead! God has done something and God is doing something ... something that our minds cannot conceive and not even the eyes of faith can fully make out. Yet he has revealed enough to assure us of his sovereign authority and call for our complete submission even now.

We would do well to remember why the church's favorite hymn is titled 'Amazing Grace' and not 'Amazing Justice'. In his mercy he has refused to give us what we deserve and in his grace he has showered us with what we cannot merit. 'Bear in mind that our Lord's patience means salvation' (2 Pet. 3:15).

Let's return to our friend Job for just a moment. Which of the seventy questions from God finally shut Job's mouth? The very first one! God began his litany of examination with: 'Who is this that darkens my counsel with words without knowledge?' (38:2). Seventy question marks later Job responded, 'I know that you can do all things; no plan of yours can be thwarted. You asked, "Who is this that obscures counsel without knowledge?" Surely I spoke of things I did not understand, things too wonderful for me to know' (42:2-3).

The question that ultimately undoes every wanna-be-king is the question about the creature's relationship to the Creator. None of us can ever ultimately get past the first question on God's test. Perhaps you have observed the bumper sticker that says, 'Just when I thought I had all the right answers, somebody switched the questions.' Maybe the questions were never switched. Could it be that I need to discover I have been asking the wrong questions all along? Reinhold Niebuhr admitted, 'There was a time when I had all the answers. My real growth began when I discovered that the questions to which I had answers were not the important questions.'[6]

Remember, putting questions to God is not wrong, questioning God is. Pondering the questions of life is sometimes the only evidence we are still alive. Our greatest struggle just might be to make certain we are asking the most important questions. We were taught in school that there are no stupid questions, but in actual fact not all questions are created equal, some are better than others. Have you been asking yourself the more valuable questions?

> Man differs from the animals in that he asks himself questions. He asks them about the world and about himself, about the meaning of things, the meaning of disease and healing, life and death. He is conscious of his weakness, of his responsibility, and of his shortcomings, and he asks himself if there is any way out. I know that it is in fact God who puts these questions to him, that it is God who is speaking to him, even though he may not realize it.[7]

Dr. Ravi Zacharias tells of talk-show host Larry King being asked what one person in all of history he would most like to interview. Mr. King answered, 'Jesus Christ.' Then the second question, 'What would you like to ask him?' The world-famous talk show host said, 'I would like to ask him if he was indeed virgin-born. The answer to that question would define history for me.'[8] I submit to you that Mr. King is beginning to ask the right kind of questions.

There is only one throne ... and God is on it. We began

with this frank assertion. I said on the opening page of our pursuit that an increasing number of our contemporaries do not buy the notion of God's absolute authority. Yet, popular or not, God is on his throne. He has no rivals. His reign has never been seriously challenged. Every stream of human history is being divinely drawn to a culminating confluence of triumph in which the majesty of his authority and the universal demonstration of his glory will thunder forth forever.

> There is a definite goal toward which history is progressing. History is not, then, merely chance happenings. And the force causing its movement is not impersonal atoms or blind fate. It is, rather, a loving God with whom we can have a personal relationship. We may look forward with assurance, then, toward the attainment of the telos of the universe. And we may align our lives with what we know will be the outcome of history.[9]

The question is not if God will win, but when. The question is not if we will submit to him, but when. The question is not if we will bow to his authority, but when.

NOTES

1. Ted Mico, ed., *Life Stinks* (Kansas City: Andrews and McMeel, 1995), pp.5-8.

2. Stuart and Doris Flexner, *The Pessimist's Guide to History* (New York: Avon Books, 1992), p.ix.

3. Warren W. Wiersbe, *Be Patient* (Wheaton, Illinois: Victor Books, 1991), pp.144-152.

4. Archibald Thomas Roberston, *Word Pictures in the New Testament* (Grand Rapids, Michigan: Baker Book House, 1931), 4:357.

5. Gordon D. Fee, *The First Epistle to the Corinthians* (Grand Rapids, Michigan: William B. Eerdmans Publishing Company, 1987), p.759.

6. Reinhold Niebuhr, quoted in Edythe Draper, *Draper's Book of Quotations For the Christian World* (Wheaton, Illinois: Tyndale House Publishers, Inc., 1992), p.515.

7. Paul Tournier, quoted in Draper, p.405.

8. Larry King, quoted in Ravi Zacharias, 'Questions I Would Like to Ask God', *Just Thinking* (Norcross, Georgia: Ravi Zacharias International Ministries, February 1998), p.1.

9. Millard J. Erickson, *Christian Theology* (Grand Rapids, Michigan: 1985), p.363.

Subject Index

Absolute/absolutes 8, 30, 39, 42, 52, 66, 69, 79, 80, 81, 101, 113, 119, 211

Abuse 13, 113-4, 120, 130, 199

Accountable/accountability 79

Administration/administrate 37, 118

Anoint/anointed 13, 35-7, 66, 90, 91170, 173

Arrogance 12, 14, 22

Assyria/Assyrians 64

Attitude 69, 108-9, 131

Attributes of God 27-30

Authority 7-8, 9, 12, 13, 25-6, 30, 34, 35, 36, 37, 44-5, 46, 49-50, 54-5, 58, 78, 79-80, 80-94, 98-9, 101-2, 105, 117-8, 124-6, 130, 132, 135-51, 153-6, 161, 175-7, 179, 181, 182, 185, 188, 191-2, 194, 200

Authority of God 8, 12, 13, 15, 22, 25-40, 41-58, 61-74, 77-94, 97-115, 117-133, 135-51, 153-73, 175-88, 191-201, 203-211

Autonomy/autonomous 8, 25, 38, 91, 130

Babylon/Babylonian(s) 64, 66, 68

Baptize/baptism 182-3, 185, 194

Call 70, 106, 153, 154, 155, 161-2, 171, 172

Child/children 7, 14, 18, 19, 26, 39, 54, 79, 8183, 85, 98, 108, 117-33, 136, 179

Church 27, 33, 44, 53, 61, 63, 65, 72, 75, 77-94, 98-9, 102, 105, 106, 115, 118, 139, 140, 142, 148, 150, 151, 153-5, 159, 161, 164, 167, 175, 176, 179, 193, 209

Church-discipline 88-9

Civil-disobedience 67-70

Consequences 13, 125

Conviction 49-51, 58

Cross 102-3, 177, 178, 191, 194, 195

Culture/cultural 9-10, 12, 17, 42, 43, 44, 78, 79, 80, 130, 144, 166, 169

Defiant/defiance 9, 13, 16, 19, 34, 130

Delegated/delegation 8, 26, 31, 33, 34, 35, 37, 42, 67, 69, 71, 74, 80, 81, 83, 84-6, 101-2, 105, 112, 113-4, 115, 118, 119, 122, 123, 125, 132, 135, 138, 142-3, 153

Demons/demonism 100, 136, 137, 143, 144-5, 146, 147, 148, 150, 178, 179

Devil 145, 146, 147, 149, 150, 201

Discern/discernment 121-2, 126, 175

Disciple/discipleship 71, 78, 126, 131, 133, 138, 182-45, 186, 187, 188, 191, 192, 195, 199, 205

Discipline 54-5, 66, 78, 83, 88-9, 120, 124, 127-80, 182, 200

Elder(s) 81, 82-4, 86, 87-91, 93, 150

Enlightenment 135

Eternal/eternity 28, 29, 31, 100, 121, 123, 151, 208

Evangelical(s) 75, 135

Father 25, 28, 31, 37, 39, 55, 80, 99, 100, 104, 108, 110, 122, 123, 126, 139, 140, 141, 150, 177, 178, 179-80, 182, 188, 206, 207

Fool/foolishness 122, 127-30, 176

Forgive/forgiveness 30, 73, 103, 115, 136, 159, 160, 161, 178

Fundamental(s)/fundamentalism 44

Glory of God 26, 27, 31, 62, 70, 73, 93, 107, 122-3, 124, 145, 151, 171, 177, 178.179, 181,   182, 194, 200, 207-8, 210

Government 13, 61-74

Grace 30, 31, 73, 92, 103, 105, 133, 145, 157, 198, 200, 209

Great Commission 80, 94, 176, 183, 184-6, 187

Head/headship 98-105, 113, 139

Hell 45, 53, 179, 187

Holy/holiness 21, 22, 26, 30, 39, 66, 72, 78, 83, 104, 105, 122, 169, 170

Humble/humility 32, 48, 51, 136, 145, 146, 177, 178, 184, 193, 200, 201

Humanist Manifesto II 39

Husband 18, 50, 98, 101-2, 104-14, 117, 150, 199

In Christ 136, 138-42, 145, 147, 148, 149, 150, 151

Independent/independence 25-6, 176, 184

Inerrancy 44, 48, 53
Jesus Seminar 42
Judge/judgement 11, 28, 35, 39, 49, 62, 66-7, 124, 171, 173, 177, 178, 186, 187, 194
Just/justice 30, 65, 69, 70, 205, 209
King/kingdom 13, 15-16, 20, 21, 28, 32, 35, 36, 37, 66-7, 68, 71, 72, 73, 85, 90, 112, 137, 139, 143, 145, 176, 179, 191, 194, 195, 196, 198, 200, 201, 206, 207, 210
Lawlessness 18
Lead/leader/leadership 77, 78, 79, 80-94, 98-9, 101, 102-5, 113, 118, 175
Liberal/liberalism 44
Millenium 114
Mother 19, 45, 50, 51, 68, 103, 110, 128, 198
Names of God 27-9
New Age 26, 47
Nike 10
Obey/obedience 14, 17-18, 20, 39, 41, 61, 67, 68, 69-70, 72, 74, 78, 81-2, 93, 97, 113, 114, 115, 125, 138, 146, 165, 182, 186, 188
Omnipotence 29, 187
Omnipresence 29
Parent/parental/parenthood 25, 85, 98, 111, 117-33, 137-8
Power 7-8, 21, 30, 31, 33, 34, 35, 52, 53, 72, 73, 75, 80, 85, 86, 87, 115, 118, 136, 138-45, 150, 151, 171, 175, 178-9, 180, 182, 186, 193, 200, 201, 204, 205, 206, 208
Pray/prayer 15, 18, 21, 30, 38, 40, 41, 54, 68, 72-3, 74, 89, 93, 138, 140, 143, 145, 146, 147, 148, 149, 150, 151, 181, 192, 194
Preach/preaching/preacher 42, 68, 81, 111, 145, 153-73, 175, 180, 182
Pride 12, 65, 66, 87, 146
Rebel/rebellion 8, 9-10, 12-22, 35, 36, 37-9, 61, 66-7, 72, 129, 131
Redeem/Redeemer/redemption 100, 177, 179
Relative/relativism 9

Repent/repentance 21, 27, 40, 72, 159, 161

Resurrection 43, 141, 159, 160, 178, 209

Rights 9, 26, 119, 161

Rome/Roman Empire 45, 63-4, 7072

Rule/reign 32, 46, 67, 81, 83, 85, 95, 179, 195, 201, 206, 210

Sacrifice/sacrificial 16, 20, 102-5, 110, 113, 115, 195, 196

Sanctify/sanctification 12, 71, 105-6, 113

Satan/Satanism 22, 38, 52, 106, 110, 136, 137, 140, 142, 143, 148-9, 150, 151, 179-80

Scripture/Word of God 13, 26, 32, 37, 39, 42, 43, 44-58, 68, 71, 77, 80-4, 86, 87, 90, 92, 106, 107, 113, 127, 130, .135, 143, 144, 148, 149, 153-73, 177, 187

Self 9, 21-2, 78, 82, 93, 103, 128, 187, 188, 196, 200, 201

Servant/servanthood 86, 102, 196, 198, 200, 205

Serve/service 85, 86, 92, 196, 200, 201

Shepherd/pastor 28, 51, 66, 83-4, 87-8, 91, 92, 93, 150, 151, 165, 168, 175, 199

Sin 11, 17, 21-2, 26, 31, 46, 49, 69, 73, 86, 103, 113, 115, 136, 140, 146, 159, 160, 171, 178, 186, 194, 209

Society 9, 61, 74, 125

Sovereign/sovereignty 8, 14, 26, 27, 28, 29, 30, 31, 33, 66, 67, 75, 83, 118, 124, 139, 171, 187, 209

Submit/submission/submissive 26, 32, 63, 65, 68, 69-70, 71-2, 74, 82, 84, 85, 91, 93, 100, 105, 107, 115, 119, 123, 124, 146, 148, 155, 179, 208, 209, 210

Sword of the Spirit 49, 156

Tax/taxation 7, 61-3, 69

Ten Commandments 43-4

Transgression 140

Trinity 99, 100, 177, 178

Universe 8, 14, 22, 25, 27, 29, 32, 33, 117, 118, 119, 121, 137, 139, 141, 177, 207

Victim/victimhood/victimization 114, 195

Victory/victorious/victor 92, 104, 136, 144, 148, 149, 151, 191

Wife 18, 83, 97-8, 101-114, 117, 142, 150

Will 14, 17-18, 41-2, 46, 66, 69, 70, 80, 81, 136-7, 141, 142, 143, 144, 147, 151, 164, 171, 178
Wise/wisdom 30, 39, 49, 73, 86, 94, 119, 121, 122, 123, 125, 126, 128-9, 130-3, 169
World 12, 23, 26, 39, 46, 57-8, 111, 123, 136, 140, 143, 146, 150, 176, 193, 201, 203, 204, 209, 210
Worship 15, 21, 30, 32, 48, 68, 139, 148, 150, 177, 195, 208
Yield/yielded/yieldedness 183-4, 187

Christian Focus Publications publishes biblically-accurate books for adults and children. The books in the adult range are published in three imprints.

Christian Heritage contains classic writings from the past.

Christian Focus contains popular works including biographies, commentaries, doctrine, and Christian living.

Mentor focuses on books written at a level suitable for Bible College and seminary students, pastors, and others; the imprint includes commentaries, doctrinal studies, examination of current issues, and church history.

For a free catalogue of all our titles, please write to
Christian Focus Publications,
Geanies House, Fearn,
Ross-shire, IV20 1TW, Great Britain

For details of our titles visit us on our web site
http://www.christianfocus.com

John Kitchen grew up on the plains of rural Iowa. After coming to faith in Christ, John sensed God's call on his life. He has served as senior pastor of the Plymouth Alliance Church, Plymouth, Wisconsin since 1987. John holds degrees from Crown College (B.A.), Columbia Biblical Seminary (M.Div.) and Trinity Evangelical Divinity School (D.Min.). His passion is communicating the timeless relevance of God's Word to this generation. He is joyfully married to Julie and together they enjoy their children Melody, Joe and Clint. John enjoys time with his family, reading, the outdoors and cycling.